Frank's Girl

Frank's Girl

Win Smith

(Winifred Prichard Smith, MBE)

The Pentland Press Limited
Edinburgh • Cambridge • Durham

First published in 1994 by
The Pentland Press Ltd.
1 Hutton Close
South Church
Bishop Auckland
Durham

ISBN 1 85821 156 5

Typeset by CBS, Felixstowe, Suffolk
Printed and bound by Antony Rowe Ltd., Chippenham

Contents

Introduction

This is the story of two large ordinary families, the Moores and the Smiths, who have very few descendants but who have instead left in their wake numerous boxes of family papers and impedimenta. This is mostly worthless, ranging as it does from Food Ration cards of the First World War to the slippers my grandmother wore at her wedding in 1872, and from funeral cards to school reports.

Before they are destroyed, I have tried to rescue those papers which will help me to paint a picture of the life I myself have known, in a Britain that has, in my lifetime, changed out of all recognition. I hope to show how it was possible for those who had no 'equality of opportunity' to climb up the educational ladder and even achieve honour in their chosen profession. Equally importantly I hope to convey some of the happiness that cocooned me in my home background, so that I was cherished and loved to the full. I have tried tempering the nostalgia with some degree of realism.

One of my personal problems, until recent years, has been to know where I fitted into society. I was brought up before the 1939 war when social status was extremely important and class divisions were based on birth and wealth. I turned into a little snob. My uncertainties as to my own status increased my basic shyness, though I welcomed every chance I could clutch of mixing with 'higher' social classes of society. My parents' position was all-important to me: my Father's University posts brought with them occasions of pomp that I found most satisfying. Between 1933 and 1947 I led a dual life with a home of considerable style, whereas my employment as a social worker was among the poor and needy. I did not do my job with any conscious feeling of patronage, and frequently tried to analyse my motivation in an effort to balance the inequality.

I was haunted as to where I was in the peck order – was I to speak with a regional accent, like some of my Father's Cheshire relations, or to speak like some of my Mother's rich relatives? (At that time I saw the former as shameful.) I never knew the answer until I was in my mid-fifties. In a Cheshire lane I met an old man I did not know, though he was a distant relative by marriage. As he shuffled past me he turned his head, and said, as a statement of fact, 'You're Frank's girl'. I watched him go, and felt a deep glow of happiness as I shouted 'Yes' after him.

That's who I really was, and am. All my bewilderment went as at last I clutched at truth and relished the comfort it brought. Now I knew who I was. Why had I ever doubted when it was all so simple? Why had it mattered? As my old friend Millie, from the Mile End Road in the East End of London, used to say, 'We are all the same, black, white, green and yellow'.

You now have freedom to assess my character. I hope you find something of interest!

THE SMITHS

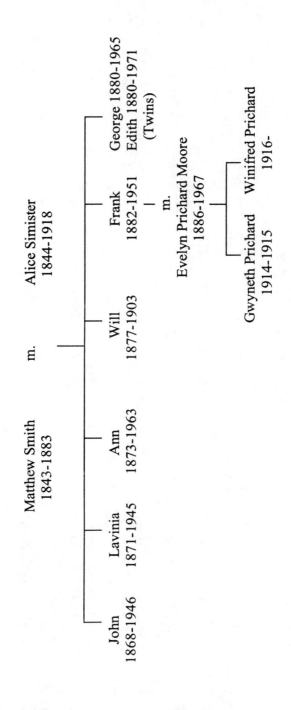

Matthew Smith
1843-1883

m.

Alice Simister
1844-1918

John
1868-1946

Lavinia
1871-1945

Ann
1873-1963

Will
1877-1903

Frank
1882-1951

George 1880-1965
Edith 1880-1971
(Twins)

m.

Evelyn Prichard Moore
1886-1967

Gwyneth Prichard
1914-1915

Winifred Prichard
1916-

THE MOORES

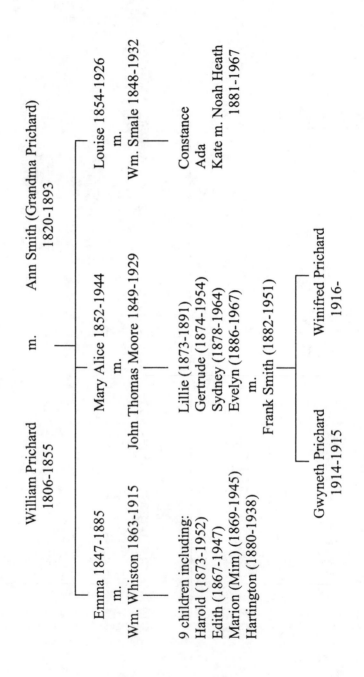

William Prichard 1806-1855   m.   Ann Smith (Grandma Prichard) 1820-1893

Emma 1847-1885
m.
Wm. Whiston 1863-1915

Mary Alice 1852-1944
m.
John Thomas Moore 1849-1929

Louise 1854-1926
m.
Wm. Smale 1848-1932

9 children including:
Harold (1873-1952)
Edith (1867-1947)
Marion (Mim) (1869-1945)
Hartington (1880-1938)

Lillie (1873-1891)
Gertrude (1874-1954)
Sydney (1878-1964)
Evelyn (1886-1967)
m.
Frank Smith (1882-1951)

Constance
Ada
Kate m. Noah Heath 1881-1967

Gwyneth Prichard 1914-1915

Winifred Prichard 1916-

Chapter One

Mary Alice Moore 1852 – 1944

Every summer we went to stay at Wood Villa, Langley, Macclesfield, with my maternal grandparents. The chief pillar of the house was my Grandmother, Mary Alice Moore. Through sickness and ever-increasing poverty she never faltered in loving God, her husband, her family, new babies and any stray animal she came across. To me she was the perfect Fairy Godmother and we adored one another. It was Heaven to drive in Bennet's taxi from Hibel Road Station in Macclesfield the three miles up through Gurnett and Langley Wood, and then to see the curving front wall of Wood Villa, with the bushes of cream lemon-scented roses over it. These had followed the lilacs that had earlier scented the road. There in the gateway – oh joy! – would be Granny, standing beaming. Behind her would be Auntie Gertie, her pince-nez wedged firmly on her nose, and Grandpa with his one arm and the beard that looked soft but was scratchy when he kissed you. Behind the reception party, yapping lustily, would be Bess, Granny's nasty little Pomeranian dog, later replaced by a series of rather stupid smooth-haired fox terriers. The hugs, the kisses, the excitement!

Then with everyone talking together at the tops of their voices we would surge into the hall with its floor of coloured geometric tiles, and the big marble-topped hatstand that, accompanied by a folding table, was eventually sold for 3/- in the saleroom in 1954, to Uncle Sydney's eternal fury. The big trunk would be carried upstairs (no lightweight luggage in those days) and we followed into the well-remembered bedrooms leading from the square landing.

After being promoted from a cot in my parents' room I was put into the little bedroom over the hall. My chief memories of it are unpleasant. It was dominated by a huge chest of drawers, still full of Great-grandma Prichard's belongings, smelling strongly of mothballs. Nothing was ever thrown away, a trait I have unfortunately inherited. Recently an unused damask tablecloth and also a double sheet surfaced in my home, both marked with the name 'Prichard' in Indian ink on the hem. These must have belonged to Grandma Prichard and been taken over with the house in 1893. Another tablecloth is similarly marked with my great-great-grandfather's name, 'I. Smith'. He died in 1850.

The bed was so narrow that more than once I fell out of it in the night. I must also have been a bed-wetter, for I can just recall the awful occasion when Auntie Gertie, a spinster with determined views, gave me a fearsome lecture on the evils of my habits and sent me to bed in a chastened mood. My father, who as a renowned educationalist had many brushes on child-rearing with her, was delighted when the next morning I got up early and immediately woke the whole house by bellowing at the top of my voice, 'Auntie Gertie, I'm wet froo!' This was a phrase Daddy cherished for years. When Grandpa died in 1929 Auntie Gertie moved into Granny's room and I was promoted to Auntie's big room which had a feather mattress on the bed. So hot in summer, but so cosy in winter, the feathers billowing round you in their snow-white cover and the stone hot water bottle heating your toes.

My parents slept across the landing in the big spare room with the rickety floor. No one ever solved the mystery of that floor. It sloped slightly, and it shook dreadfully when you tiptoed across it. Mother always prophesied it would end in doom and disaster, and was really scared of it. Once Grandfather drove a big iron bar through the outside wall of the house, and in under the floorboards, but this only made the shaking worse, so after a year or two he got the bar out

2

again.

By the bed there was Grandma Prichard's sewing table, each little compartment under the octagonal lid with treasures tucked in it – a little box of tiny pink shells gathered on Blackpool and Southport beaches (Granny called them babies' fingernails), a miniature ivory domino set, quaint pincushions, a smelling salts bottle in vivid blue glass, and medals in honour of Charles Wesley and Queen Victoria. I have them all still and they never fail to remind me of the special trip Granny and I took upstairs each summer to explore all the contents and to gloat over them.

Granny's bedroom looked over the fields to the back garden and hills. It was always important to know if the cows were on top of Pyegreave, or on its slopes, so that one knew if it was going to rain or not. She had a dressing table and wardrobe which had round crystal handles, cut in the shape of flowers. By the bed, on Grandpa's side, stood his watch holder: every night he hung his pocket watch there so that he could see it from where he lay. All the bedrooms of course had marble-topped washstands and very pretty flowered toilet sets – Mother's room had also a mini-ewer and basin for rose-water.

On the landing stood the Broom. This was always there in summer, for there was a family hatred of large moths, or buzzards as we called them. It was impossible to read in bed without attracting them in from outside: they then made frenzied dashes at the candle and at the luckless occupants of a bed, who would be cowering under the sheet, only one eye peering out to see whether the moth was going to hit or miss. Most summer nights I would be lying peacefully in bed in the dark, just going off to sleep, when a startled scream would come from the passage outside – Mother: she liked reading in bed, and she was the most vociferous of the family – she would push my loudly protesting father out of bed, the bedroom door would fly open, the Broom would be grabbed, and the long kill would take place. Crashes, bangs, screams and vituperations reverberated round the house until victory was achieved, and the Broom was restored to its corner on the landing until the next sufferer wanted it.

3

Downstairs meals would appear ceaselessly on the big dining room table. Always, at my request, there was one of Granny's lovely home-cooked tongues, which was 'on the cut'. But it was the amount and vastness of the fruit that made every meal special. The garden of Wood Villa's 1,878 square yards abounded in fruit: at any one time there would be stewed morello cherries, morello pie, gooseberry pie, raspberry pie, fresh raspberries, stewed raspberries and red and black currant tarts. Later in the season came fresh jargonelle pears and victoria plums, all bursting with juice, and followed into the house by a string of besotted wasps. Custards were made with fresh eggs and a leaf of lemon verbena for flavour. Thick cream was fetched in jugs from Mrs Bullock at the Hall Farm next door. Dear Polly Bullock! How I loved her as she clattered in clogs round her stone-flagged dairy, and sometimes, as a treat, took me into her kitchen. A covered basket in front of the fire meant that as soon as I pulled the cloth off it a cloud of bright yellow baby chickens scattered all over the floor, cheeping with delight. I had to corral them again in the basket before I left in case a cat got them or anyone stood on them.

The larder at Wood Villa was down a steep flight of stone stairs leading to the two cellars. Shelves, high above your head, had been put across the steps, so that a lot of the food was kept there in a cool draught. As Grannie and Auntie Gertie got older this rather dangerous place was used less, and the bowls of pies and fruit were left on the vast marble mantelpiece of the dining room. Mother refused ever to take anything to the cellar – she had been brought up on the story of how Grandma Prichard had accidentally dropped her baby brother William Smith (born in 1825) down similar steps at Bollin House, Langley. As a result he was lame all his life. He was a tape manufacturer, and his fame lay in strengthening Methodism in Langley.

My Great Grandmother Prichard really needs a book to herself. Born Ann Smith on 29th August 1820 at Hole House, Langley, she married Great Grandpa William Prichard of Manchester at Prestbury Church on 23rd October 1844, before catching a stage coach to London for the honeymoon. They had five children, of whom three reached maturity – Emma, Mary Alice and Louisa. The oldest girl, Elizabeth Ann ('Lilly'), born in Stock Street, Cheetham, Manchester in 1845, died on June 2nd 1863. A son, Edward William, died when a day old, in 1850, at Langley. Grandpa Prichard died on 2nd February 1855, aged 48 years.

Grandma Prichard was a very dominant widow, ruling the family and the village with great firmness. (My cousin, Will Moore, in recent years said he was sure she still ruled the family). Certainly the possessions she left behind her were venerated, and large numbers of her relatives had her surname incorporated in their own names. In her portrait, supposedly painted when she was 18 years old, the face is mature and stern. She was wealthy, but in her last years she had to be restrained from giving eternal cheques to East End Missions and to anybody who wrote asking her for help. A principal task of Granny's eldest daughter, Lily Moore, was to try to control the money, for during the last three years of her short life she lived as Grandma Prichard's companion.

Uncle Sydney was obviously in awe of his Grandma Prichard. For some childish ailment she once put a very large poultice on his chest, with mustard half an inch thick on it. However, she did not believe in idleness: before the garden path at Wood Villa was asphalted, it was his job to kneel with a table fork and get the little weeds out of the gravel. Grandma Prichard came out of the house every quarter of an hour to see it was well done and to talk to him about his soul and ultimate destination. This work frequently ended in tears.

The house, Wood Villa, was full of family history. Once, when being burgled, Grandma Prichard had rung her big dinner bell out of an upstairs window in order to get help; the robber was apprehended by local men on the Hollins before he reached Macclesfield. She then had the back door lined with sheet iron – this made it a tremendous weight, and every night it was solemnly locked and bolted at dusk by Auntie Gertie. The fact that the front door stood hospitably open to all hours was immaterial (in any case, if shut and locked all the village knew that the key was kept under the foot scraper standing outside the

5

front door). The downstairs rooms all had deep wooden shutters that folded into the wall: again those on the dining-room window at the back of the house and in the front breakfast room were closed and barred each night – but not the front drawing-room window. It was in the dining-room that Grandma Prichard conducted family prayers each morning, praying the same prayers each day for the fifteen years that Uncle Sydney attended.

Our holidays were fun. First of all there was always the rockery to explore. A venerable toad lived under the rockery steps, and most years there was a wasps' nest to investigate in the rockery. Then there was the debate as to who was to pick the jargonelle pears. The tree stood about sixty feet high (or so it seemed) and the long pole with the net on the end (made by Grandpa) would not reach the topmost fruit. This meant the gatherer had to climb a tall step ladder that gave an inexplicable lurch when you got high on it – so much so that it had jerked Grandma Prichard off in the last century and she had broken her leg. Mother always became faintly hysterical if my father offered to use these steps, and sternly forbade it, so it fell to Auntie Gertie's lot to mount aloft, holding the pole in one hand, and wobbling dangerously. When I dismantled the house in 1954 I insisted that this innocent-looking but lethal flight of steps be destroyed, otherwise I am sure they would still be unexpectedly throwing their user to the ground.

Let us continue exploring the garden. Grandpa uprooted the pink moss roses on the house wall in order to plant espalier plums, but there is a white jasmine to sniff, and two kinds of honeysuckle that smothered the holly hedge near the back door, and which discreetly hid the path that led to the three-seater loo down the yard. On down the garden and then out through the gate in the wall at the bottom, which led into the fields. If it had been raining and the cows had been up to the wall, there were great muddy ruts to skip over, and cowpats to avoid before you crossed the field and slithered carefully down the steep slope to the brook. This was the Bollin, where my cousin Bun and I had sailed the little toy boat kept specially for grandchildren. On days when Langley Print Works were dyeing silk the water would be wondrously coloured and smelly. This was because the dyeing of the silk was done with colours produced from plants and fixed or fastened by use of a mordant obtained from farm manure. Animal excreta was collected from shippon and field for the madder printed styles that Langley was famous for.

Then over the little wooden bridge which in 1882 gave way under Uncle Sydney, so that he fell in and cut his head open. He was carried on his father's shoulders back up to Grandma Prichard's at Wood Villa to be dried and bandaged. She gave him musk drops and Indian Rock to eat – a great delight. After the bridge, up the steep bank and then the long horizontal walk along the Hollins to Macclesfield, with its haunting views of the Cheshire Plain. Granny and I knew a certain stone up there that had a prolific wild strawberry plant growing round it, and her bonnet bounced on her head as she helped me to gather the crop each year. She wore bonnets until she died in 1944: they were made exclusively for her by one milliner in Macclesfield, and she firmly refused to wear a hat.

The last time I did this walk was in 1953 and it was Sunday evening. I was staying with my father's sisters at 285 Buxton Road, Macclesfield, and had been up all day at Wood Villa with Auntie Gertie who was lying ill with heart and breathing problems, besides endless difficulties over employing carers. I knew she was deteriorating. I climbed up the hill and stood looking down at Langley and the lovely valley of the Bollin. I could just see Wood Villa's roof and chimneys in the trees. The warm evening sunshine lit up the valley with startling clarity, and sharpened all the shadows. There was no sound except for the occasional sheep bleating on Ward's Knob, and a large and a late bee buzzing among the harebells at my feet. Across the great Cheshire plain I could hear faint church bells, calling the faithful to service. I stood there and the tears cascaded down my face. I had suddenly realised that this was the end of an era, and that soon the Prichards and the Moores and the Whistons would all be gone from Langley, after all those years when they had been part of the very structure of a community whose lives had been so closely interwoven. That soft evening air and those impressions are for ever imprinted on my mind – I still feel warmed by the beauty of it all, as I remember the love that had always encircled me, and the joy I got from being part of the family.

Other early memories are of being allowed to climb up and ride on the top of the haycart when it went laden down to the farm. Granny always sent jugs of her special lemonade or lemon balm tea across to the haymakers working in the field across the road from Wood Villa and I helped to carry them. Horses were of course the main transport in those days – very few cars came to the village, except for Auntie Whiston's limousine and chauffeur. When I was small we always used to walk into Macclesfield, when going to tea with my father's sisters Annie, Edith and Vinnie. I can just remember being pushed there in my pushchair – a wonderful wooden upright affair with a small footboard for the feet, on which my little button boots rested. I was inordinately proud of the floorboard because it was covered with a small strip of Granny's drawing-room carpet (hideous yellowy-green in colour, with a pattern of faded pink cabbage roses on it). I felt this carpet gave me enormous status, and I used to point my stubby little nose as high as it would go in the air, as my equipage whirled along the dusty footpath.

Minor and major illnesses seemed to be unending in my Grandmother's time, for nearly every postcard (sent daily) and letter refers to someone's health. 'Mother is still in bed: hope she will be down tomorrow'; 'Eve (staying at Blackpool to recuperate) has not fainted today, think she may get up tomorrow'; 'Am sending you a chicken – do eat properly'.

Stomach upsets, influenza, acute and perpetual coughs and fevers in the family are paralleled by messages from contemporaries, many speaking of selfless day and night home nursing. 'Papa spoke two words to us today: such a comfort to Mama'. Devoted daughters thought nothing of giving up their lives to elderly and failing parents.

If anything serious was suspected, another member of the family rushed to the sufferer's side (shades of Elizabeth Bennett in *Pride and Prejudice!*). Auntie Gertie went to my Mother, who was staying with the cousins at Ellenhall: Grandpa, not speaking a word of German, tore off to Uncle Sydney's side when he was being operated on in Jena, and so it goes on. But Uncle Sydney, in his later years coping with near nervous breakdowns from overwork, thrombosis, a shattering cough, gallstones, and also my Mother, racked with chest complaints in Leeds fogs, her ever present arthritis, and becoming a house-bound invalid for the last seven years of her life, both lived past the eighty mark, doubtless helped by their family's earlier responses to their physical frailties.

Granny, who only gave up playing cricket with me when she was eighty years old, and who suffered from many minor ailments, lived to be ninety-two. I was once in Wood Villa when she was in her late eighties and was obviously ill, so Mother insisted the doctor was sent for. To her horror she then learnt the General Practitioner was still Dr Somerville, who had brought all Granny's children into the world and who had been a great family friend. He duly arrived, too frail to walk, and was half-carried into the hall by his chauffeur. He sat on the settle near the front door with Granny, and they had a lovely little chat about the old days. Then he said: 'You'll do, Polly,' and gave her a prescription and his chauffeur carried him out again to his car. 'I feel much better,' said Granny, looking a transformed being. 'That man will kill you, Mother,' said my Mother gloomily. 'It's time you got a younger doctor.'

'Certainly not,' said Granny. 'He understands me.'

Chapter Two

John Thomas Moore, 1846 – 1929

J.T. Moore, son of Thomas (1805 – 1878) and Ann Moore (1818 – 1886) was born on 3rd July 1846 at Blakenhall, Cheshire. He was the eldest of seven children and did not become a farmer, like his father. He was educated locally at Wrinehill where he was taught by an old veteran of Wellington's Army who was keen on discipline and who caned the soles of JTM's feet. He learnt little. Later he was apprenticed to Thornleys, Linen and Wool Drapers of Earl Street, Crewe, where he boarded, and worked half the night on his books. His health broke down, and he went home for a year and never attempted to study after that.

JTM's brother, William, was a famous cheese maker, winning prizes in London: his brother Ernest, equally famous, supplied cheese to the House of Lords. JTM's youngest brother, Peter, (1866 – 1941) farmed on his own account at Ellenhall Park, Eccleshall from 1881 to 1934. Another brother, Joseph (1849 – 1935) emigrated to New Zealand and farmed successfully there. The brothers always kept in close touch with one another.

JTM never lost interest in the work of his father's farm, and as late as 1884 he won a silver medal at the Wirral and Birkenhead Agricultural Society's Show for an 'Ensilager', and in 1885 a silver medal from the Cheshire Agricultural Society at Crewe for 'Corn Grinding Mills, Chaff Cutters, Pulpers etc.' Ten years later medals began to be given to him for folding chairs: in 1894 the Altringham Agricultural Society's

11

very lovely medal 'For Collection of Patent Adjustable Chairs' and in 1896 the Wirral and Birkenhead Agricultural Society's medal 'For Patent Folding Chairs'.

On the 11th March 1872 JTM married, at Brunswick Chapel, Macclesfield, Mary Alice Prichard (1852 – 1944) of Langley. She was the granddaughter of Isaac Smith, and sister of Mrs William Whiston, and of Mrs William Smale, all well-known names in the silk trade. My grandfather had little to offer her financially: by then he had become a draper, with a large shop and house at Sutton House, Mill Lane, Macclesfield. He was a restless man, full of ideas, with a sense of humour, and although Granny adored her handsome husband, as a breadwinner he was a failure. The shop did not prosper and in 1883 he moved her and their three children, Lillie (1873 – 1891) Gertrude Alice (1874 – 1954) and Sydney Herbert (1878 – 1964) to Crewe, where he got a large draper's shop in Victoria Street. This also ended in disaster, and he then started a tiny shop there at the bottom of High Street. In 1886 my mother, Evelyn Prichard Moore, was born at their home at 48, Cemetery Road, Crewe, the only one of the children not born at Langley: Sydney teased her about this all her life – he had hated living in Crewe.

Initially they had a maid there called Lizzie, who is recorded as saying that she never got on well with a Monday unless she had the weekly washing done (by hand for five people) by 8 a.m. JTM was in great poverty: his wife is recorded as bursting into tears because she could not give her son 1d for a lump of 'Hokey Cokey' when he asked for it. All the family used to go to a Public Meat Market Auction at 10 p.m. on a Saturday night to buy a joint of meat. To make a little money Grandpa started selling rennet to farmers in the Haslington, Sandbach, Wybunbury and Nantwich districts, and walked round the farms. He often took his young son Sydney with him: the boy had been very ill with scarlet and rheumatic fever, and JTM always believed in the beneficial powers of fresh air. He thought nothing of walking the three miles each way into Macclesfield from Langley, often twice in one day, and on July 14th, 1927, at the age of eighty-one years he walked to Buxton and back – twelve miles each way.

Red letter days were when Grandma Prichard, (Granny's mother) visited them in Crewe, bringing with her a white chip basket full of raspberries, currants and gooseberries from the Langley garden, so that the children, who had almost forgotten such delights, imagined themselves Rajahs and Ranees at a feast. In 1887 the whole family moved back to Langley, where they were given the use of a house called The Firs. Grandma Prichard then lived at Wood Villa, and doled out largesse; it was often Sydney's task on his way home from school to carry a large rice pudding from there up to The Firs, and also his heavy and fractious baby sister, Evelyn. On one terrible occasion, struggling along with the load, he dropped the pudding and broke the dish.

The chair-making business was now being built up by Grandpa, and he was displaying his skill as an inventor. He took over the Bollin Head Mill at Langley: this was always called the Tape Mill, from the days when Isaac Smith (his wife's grandfather) used it for manufacturing tapes. Distinctive letterheads, postcards and illustrated leaflets about the patent folding chairs are still in existence. ('Moore's Chairs: a Recherché Wedding Gift'). They were built in solid walnut, with brass actions, and upholstered in the best Wilton Pile. The leaflets carry testimonials on the back pages, praising their comfort, and written by such people as the then Mayor of Macclesfield, Dr Somerville, JP, FRCS, LRCP (the family doctor) and William Whiston, JP (JTM's brother-in-law) besides various unknown but grateful individuals. Some of the folding chairs rocked:

'The peculiar wave-like motion (totally unlike that produced by any other chair) when using it makes it valuable for those with sluggish and constipated bowels. Its action is perfect massage without the toilsome labour, and as prevention is better than cure, the daily use of its gentle undulatory motion will greatly assist the liver and bowels in securing that vigorous health which is of so much value to everyone.'

This frankness was later toned down into:

'Few realise how beneficial the gentle rocking of the body is to the system. It is undoubtedly a great help to digestion. It is soothing to the nerves, lulls and composes to sleep, and gives needed support and recuperation to the tired and jaded body.'

Other chairs were advertised as 'Best Ship or Lawn Tennis Chairs' and testimonials were printed from all over the country as the chairs began to reach a wide market. Pictured sitting in them, in the leaflets, are JTM himself, or one of his family – his daughter Evelyn (my mother) looking the most rebellious. However it was a close and loving family, and there was great family support for the venture, especially for the Patent Bar Lock chair. Patents were given by the Patent Office for Folding Chairs in 1886, 1902 and 1910, and there was a Patent in 1909 for 'Moore's improvements in Bed Rests'.

At the least separation the Moore family wrote prodigiously to one another and specialised in despatching postcards to Langley from every corner of the British Isles. Even though great mounds of correspondence were burnt when Wood Villa was sold in 1954 (the family had moved there from The Firs in 1893, when Grandma Prichard died), sixty-three postcards were rescued which had been sent by JTM to his family during the time when he was rushing round the country selling his chairs to furniture firms.

This form of nomadic life seemed to suit Grandpa's restless temperament, and his postcards (while they also contain coded references to sales) usually add comments on weather, the countryside and interesting sights worth seeing. While JTM was on his travels his wife and eldest daughter, Gertie, acted as unpaid secretaries passing on mysterious directions to his employees at the mill. Underlying it all, though, was a certain lack of stability in his impetuosity: his daughter Evelyn used to recall how, once when she was a young teenager, he took her to Liverpool for the day, and suddenly decided that they would go on to the Isle of Man, so he rushed her on board a ship. They got back to Langley the next day where his wife, nearly demented with anxiety at the lack of news, awaited them. The voyage had been stormy and Evelyn, for a week afterwards, always had to dart out of the room when any food was put on the table for a meal. She never again went to the Isle of Man.

At last it looked as if Grandpa's ship was moving into calmer waters as the orders for chairs came in. In July 1911, however, whilst doing maintenance at the water wheel in the Mill, his left arm got caught in the machinery and was broken in eight places. It was amputated at Macclesfield Infirmary. Bollin Head Mill does not appear to have finally closed until 1926, for handicap did not dim Grandpa's inventive powers. Records from the Patent Office show his 'improvements in Adjustable Chairs' was patented in 1913, and again in 1916 his specification for 'Adjustable Seats for Carriages and Other Vehicles' is recorded. In 1923 'improvements in Tables, Chairs and Desks' was patented. An undated letter to his daughter Evelyn (my Mother) refers to this latter Patent:

> 'Have invented a new table that folds into small space which should be a consideration in poky rooms. A table of 35 x 45 takes up 35 x 6 and stands up when folded. What'll be my next prank before I kick the bucket, perhaps a change-speed gear, we'll see.'

In 1926 Harold Whiston, (JTM's nephew by marriage) bought the stock and tools of the Mill for £122.18.11d. In JTM's papers is the draft of the letter he wrote to my Cousin Harold on that occasion:

> 'Dear Harold,
> I herewith enclose the key of the Mill. I regret that your kind wishes and desires for me and mine should have so

15

poor a result, and tho' I have long thought I might win thro' to prosperity I feel that my handicaps now preclude so desirable a success. The machinery will be at your own valuation. List before depreciation in white book at the shop.'

After that Grandpa had a tiny workshop in the garden of Wood Villa and there, with infinite patience and the aid of a good vice, he continued to do carpentry with one arm. He was a staunch teetotaller and a deeply religious man, being closely associated with Langley Wesleyan Chapel from 1887. There he served both as a steward and trustee, and he was a Sunday School teacher there for over thirty years. The Chapel remained his chief interest until his death in 1929, aged eighty-three years. At one time he was a fellow of the Royal Horticultural Society and did much pioneer work propagating fruit trees in the Wood Villa garden, once having six different kinds of apples grafted on one stock, and all fruiting simultaneously. There is still in existence a crown of rhubarb he brought back from a Royal Show in the last century, and which is like no other rhubarb. The huge stems dissolve into delicious green fluff with practically no cooking at all.

Grandpa became a silent and stern figure. The very handsome young man, full of ideas, who had sung duets at the piano in the Mill Lane home, who had a keen sense of humour, and who got his son to teach him how to ride a penny farthing bicycle in 1885, had often found life harsh. As a family provider he had been a failure: often he had to live on his wife's extremely slender means and accept charity from her family, and although they doubtless recognised his honesty they were exasperated by his inability to make a success of any job. His love for those around him and his faith never faltered, though his courage must have been very stretched at times. His daughter Evelyn, in a vague effort to explain his bad luck, always comforted herself by saying that he had been born in the wrong age. Even his devoted wife, who spoke ill of no one, wrote to her daughter when he died, 'Oh how

16

I shall miss him, but he was a great trial to us, and I was cross with him, but he'll welcome me Home.' She rejoiced that 'the whole village and countryside paid Daddy homage: the respect shown was wonderful.'

Grandpa himself wrote to his children when he became eighty years old: 'It's lovely to find that after all the crudities and mistakes of life, there is such a thing as love, and because you all have such a stock of it my path is on enchanted land. I can never thank you as I ought for all the good things I haven't deserved. My octogenarian days I want to make as bright as I can: there are possibilities at hand if I had only vision and sense to secure them again. I thank you for the expression of love you have shown, Much love to all. Ever yours, JT Moore.'

At his Golden Wedding in 1922 his wife had not expected a present from him, so she was deeply moved when he put his hand under his pillow and gave her a doctor's bill she had been worried about paying. It was duly receipted: he had made a chair secretly in his workshop and sold it. It was actions like this that made his son call him the most honourable and kind-hearted man he had ever known.

Chapter Three

Gertrude Alice Moore 1874 – 1954

Through all her troubles and poverty Granny's love of her fellows, both poor and rich, shone out. She welcomed and loved them and her generosity was well-known: no one ever left the house without a bag of fruit or a spray of flowers from the garden. In winter it might be a pot of home-made jam, or a drink of her home-made blackberry cordial which she always said was non-alcoholic, but which periodically exploded in the chiffonier where it was stored. Life dealt her some harsh blows. She had seven children: the oldest, Lillie, died at the age of eighteen years from appendicitis, old Dr Somerville desperately trying to save her by attaching twenty leeches to her stomach. (This daughter had been called after Granny's beloved older sister who had also died tragically young at the age of eighteen years.) Then her second daughter, Gertrude, got rheumatic fever when they lived in Crewe, and got frightening quinseys at times. Her only son, Sydney Herbert, had smallpox and chicken-pox in Crewe, and five operations on an elbow joint between 1897 and 1904, when the tubercular joint was finally removed in Jena. My mother, Evelyn Prichard, had a tubercular ankle for several years, and I have already mentioned the loss of Grandpa's arm. In spite of all this Granny emerged smiling and happy with her lot, and she never faltered in her love for her family.

Her main home prop, especially in later years, was Gertrude. Auntie Gertie was intensely religious, and from 1892 was for fifty-four years a Sunday School teacher in the Macclesfield Methodist Circuit. She became a local preacher in 1921, going through storm and flood to preach in various chapels in the hills round Macclesfield. She was president of Langley Methodist Women's Meeting and a lifelong worker for overseas missions. She once had a proposal of marriage from a Minister going overseas as a missionary. She was much troubled as to where her duty lay, but after consulting all her relatives she decided she should stay at home. This she always did, except for holidays. However, like all young ladies of her generation, she had built up a 'bottom drawer' of items earmarked for when she married and set up her own home. Soon after she was seventy years old she broke it up: I came in for a silver salt cellar in the shape of a swan, which was subsequently stolen by one of our maids.

She was slap-dash – always rushing, slamming doors, making cakes that one never knew whether they would rise or fall, cutting the grass, digging up potatoes, whirring away at ill-shaped garments on her old hand sewing machine, visiting the sick. 'Miss Moore's so good at a death-bed,' said one villager to my Mother.

She was very kind – sometimes mistakenly so. Once when we were returning home she kept trying to give us more and more jars of jam and a bag of ripe home-grown tomatoes someone had given her. They finally disappeared, and she quietened down, which roused my Mother's suspicions. At the time my Father was writing his life of Sir James Kay-Shuttleworth, and had with him, on loan, a trunk of papers from the Shuttleworth archives. Mother threw open the box. There, shoved inside, was the squashy bag of tomatoes. A terrific row ensued, which reduced Auntie Gertie to tears, but thank Heaven the papers arrived back at Aberystwyth in pristine condition.

Like all the family Auntie Gertie was a great sender of letters, and in particular of postcards. Some of them give clues to her lifestyle, as the one in 1905 to her mother, posted at Crewe Station. 'I have brought my watch key but alas have forgotten my watch, but perhaps I can manage without.' About the same time another one, addressed to my Mother, bore the stirring message: 'Dear Eve. I don't think Florence will like these corduroy knickers. They are to be sure to have cloth bands to button round the knees. If you go into town again I wonder if you could see if they have any of this sort. Size 4 and then we will return these. They were 2/11d. Get them on appro and then we will return these tomorrow night.' There was a family belief that all postmen read postcards (I wonder what they should have made of the above example), so often Uncle Sydney wrote key words backwards so as to floor them. He also burst into French and German, in which he was highly skilled, so that, together with the fact that he and my Mother wrote almost illegibly, makes it a slow and difficult task deciphering some of the gems they wrote.

Auntie Gertie was much given to shouting encouragement: 'Lay a good foundation, Win!', she kept roaring at breakfast when I was toying with a cup of tea and a slice of toast. (She believed in bacon and eggs and no nonsense). Whenever I go for a walk I can hear the faint echo of that well-known voice floating behind me. 'Now, Win, open your pipes'. My chief terror of her was that, on each holiday, she would interrogate me about the state of my religious beliefs. I could always see it coming, and we played cat and mouse as I tried to avoid being hemmed in a corner and forced to discuss my more private thoughts. Her opening gambit was always the same. 'Do you love Jesus, Win?' To a shy adolescent such direct attacks are embarrassing and I curled up under the ruthless interrogation that followed. My parents were fully aware of all this, and from the sidelines used to watch with keen appreciation all my efforts to avoid being caught, my father shaking with silent laughter. Although intensely religious himself, and never losing his own faith and standards, he never tried to instill in me – or anyone else – religious dogma. It was simply unspoken faith in our house.

Another of Auntie Gertie's habits was to blow her nose with a deafening trumpeting sound. This always seemed to happen as we were all listening to the nine o'clock news on Granny's antique radio. The door would crash open on the dot of nine, heralding Auntie Gertie's entry into the breakfast room. She would pick up the daily paper, or the *Methodist Recorder*. She read it by shaking and folding the pages impatiently, getting them to the right angle to pick up the light from the hissing gas incandescence in the middle of the room. The aged radio was much given to inexplicable fadings, as its wet batteries were never of the best, so it was important to concentrate if one wanted to learn what the national news was. However, before long, the nose trumpeting would start, reducing my Mother to furious shouts, Granny, Daddy and I, to suppressed chortles. (I inherited something similar in that my sneezes, when they come, are earth shattering, and have been known to stop a committee meeting dead. They are known to my friends as 'Smith Specials.')

After Granny died in 1944 Auntie Gertie continued to live in Wood Villa alone. She developed heart trouble, and a series of people were brought into the house to look after her. I went over and rearranged the house for her, so that the carers had a private sitting room, but in her loneliness she gave them no peace. She pattered in and out of their room, clad in a dressing gown, and always talking and arousing resentment. In 1954 her doctor, a brisk and insensitive man who had never heard of gerontology, told me she was 'a pest', but that we should have her to live with us in Newcastle upon Tyne. By then my widowed mother was housebound with arthritis, and I was working full-time. In any case to uproot Auntie Gertie in her late seventies from a home where she had lived since 1893 would not have answered. Life to her was her involvement with the village, generation by generation. 'Let her brother take her,' then said the doctor. Poor Uncle Sydney was at the time living with his bedfast wife in his son's house in Oxford, and although Auntie Gertie doted on him he also was in no position to help – except that he was so angry with the doctor he wanted to report him to the British Medical Association.

I went over as often as I could. One of the most pathetic sights I have ever seen was Auntie Gertie in a hospital ward in 1954, sitting up in bed, watching the door for someone to come and visit her. She was always watching and waiting: one suspects for the past, long since dead, for she discounted all those who did come to see her. Uncle Sydney was perceptive in his analysis of it all, writing that 'In

22

1944 Gertie had lost a mother she had always known. She got some compensation in chapel meetings and corporate feeling, but when in 1950 the doctors stopped her restless peregrinations round the neighbourhood she developed a hunted expression. Ordered to sit down and keep her legs up made no impression on her loneliness. People urging her to do less only added fuel to her basic unhappiness.'

In some ways Auntie Gertie's character was as complex as that of her father. She was the oldest child in the family, relied on by her parents to set an example to the others, and at all times to live by Christian principles. This must have clashed with her jealousy of the rich cousins, yet she had interesting and stimulating friends of her own, and in her youth was a skilled artist and avid reader of good literature. In spite of frequent travels in this country, and at least two trips abroad, she remained very insular in outlook. Even so she could surprise me. I remember once when we were all out on a country walk we disturbed a young couple locked in one another's arms in a hayfield. She identified them as youngsters she knew. She only pulled a wry face at my mother, when I had expected a lecture on sin.

Chapter Four

Sydney Herbert Moore 1878 – 1974

Uncle Sydney was born on Easter Sunday, 21st April – or twenty days too late, as my Mother always told him. His father was then thirty-two and his mother twenty-six years old and they already had Lillie (five) and Gertie (three and a half).

Uncle Sydney was a lively lad. At the age of two years he killed a cat. History does not recount how he did this; his own chief memory being of how his mother wept. At the age of four years he was given a penknife on his birthday – it was taken away the same day from his bleeding hands. At his first school where he was taken by his older sisters, he brought shame on them by pouring the full contents of a blue inkwell down the inside back collar of a girl wearing a 'swell new blue velvet frock' and whom he had christened 'Proud Doll'.

1883 was the momentous year when the family moved to Crewe. Uncle's new school there made him learn twenty words a night out of his spelling book, and he won his first prize, *Johnny, Lessons for Little Boys*. He also carried out there his first scientific experiment. In his father's shop in Victoria Street there was a glass floor in the upstairs Hat Department in order to light the counter below. So as to test the strength of the glass, Uncle attacked it with a hammer. The glass broke, falling on the counter, the customer, and his father below. Perhaps this was why in later years he turned his talents to the safer world of the arts.

The children were often ill in Crewe; Uncle Sydney had scarlet fever and rheumatic fever there in 1883, with four doctors in attendance, one of whom said Uncle would not live twenty-four hours more. It left him with a deaf left ear and a weak right arm. He also had smallpox, chicken-pox (three times), pleurisy and measles (twice). Gertie had rheumatic fever. Convalescence was usually at Ellenhall Park, Staffs., where Grandpa's parents farmed. However, on June 6 1886 my Mother, Evelyn Prichard Moore, was born. 'A really pretty baby' wrote Uncle Sydney. He approved of her because he often had to finish some of her rusks and milk. In 1887 the family moved back to Langley, Macclesfield, to a house called The Firs which belonged to Granny's relatives. It was a detached house, with four bedrooms. It had no drinking water inside: all had to be carried in a large pail from a tap in the wall of the road outside. Nor was there indoor sanitation. The garden had many Tom Putt apple trees, and a swing. Lillie, Gertie and Sydney walked daily the three miles into Macclesfield to attend the Congregational School in Townley Street. Sydney learnt there quantities of English verse, ranging from Thomas Moore to Marmion. Discipline was strict: the sinister words 'Stand Out' meant a scholar left his desk and stood with his toes on the chalk line that was drawn in front of every class. Periodically the headmaster came along with his cane and sampled it on all those toeing the line. Pens, pencils, rulers etc. were given out at the start of each class, and collected at the end.

In 1890 Uncle Sydney won a scholarship (gaining 815 marks out of a possible 1,000) to King Edward VI Grammar School, Macclesfield. This school had branched off in 1844 from the old Grammar School, founded in 1498, but they were re-amalgamated in 1910. Uncle always remembered the masters and their degrees of proficiency. The headmaster believed in correlating subjects, so Euclid and Geography were learnt from French textbooks. In 1891 Uncle won a prize for good conduct, but the year was dominated by the death of his oldest sister, Lillie, aged eighteen years. The death hit the family very hard, and she was always venerated by her siblings. At the funeral her coffin was smothered in Marechal Niel roses, sent by Uncle Whiston from his hot houses, and Uncle Sydney, with mixed pride, wore his first pair of trousers.

In 1893 Uncle – by now called Shem by his friends – started as a pupil teacher back at Townley Street School. The following year he also became Hon. Secretary of the Langley Institute, and at once took steps to increase its membership. For £12 he bought a half-sized billiard table in Bolton, and started running courses in Hen Culture, Gardening, etc., all of which proved popular. By now, too, he was having articles and verses published, and in the December he made his first visit to London, mainly to attend religious meetings, but also to see the sights. In 1896 he became friends with William Simister Smith, my father's oldest brother, who came to regard Langley as his second home. When Will won a scholarship to Owen's College (Manchester University) his letters kept Shem *au courant* with his studies so that, in a sense, they were doing the same training.

Shem's next job was as teacher at Priory House, Bridlington, from 1896 – 98. There he learnt to row and steer a boat with one arm, sat his senior Oxford examination, and fell in love with (subsequently marrying in 1904) the Headmaster's daughter, Florence Gibson. Next he became fourth master at Victoria College, Congleton, for less than a year, when he left to have operations both on his left ear and his weak right arm. This was broken and reset, resulting in seven years of great pain. In 1899 he was for two months headmaster of Wildboarclough Elementary School, near Macclesfield – a seven mile walk each way, and he had to be there by 9 a.m. He had thirty scholars in six standards to teach, and the help of one female assistant, aged sixteen years. He always said that his hardest task was to teach the girls knitting.

In September 1899 he sailed in the *Albatross* from Tower Bridge for Bordeaux. Landing there at 8 p.m. he succeeded in being arrested by the police at 10 p.m. the same night, having got locked in a park of wild animals by accident. He was en route to the Dordogne, there to teach and improve his French at the *École Primaire Superieure et Professionelle.* Colourful postcards and letters flowed home – he had seen a donkey dying in the street after it was bitten by a scorpion. He had caught and cooked snakes – 'very good'. He went truffle hunting with the headmaster's large dog, who when she found a truffle could only be hauled away from the site by her six inch stub of a tail. Cycling near Nontron in the February he saw his first wolf. These wolves were a godsend to him, and later to my father, for both at times wrote articles on Wolves in France that were published in the *Manchester Guardian*. By June Uncle was listening to the nightingales singing all round him. Then he was off on his travels – first to La Rochelle, and next, in August, to Lisbon, where he found life was still exciting as he just missed seeing a garotting. (Instead he saw the vultures flying overhead). He reached Badajoz in great heat, where 'swearing parrots and hungry mosquitoes' disturbed his nights, but he enjoyed eating frogs for the first time. In the September he was again arrested: this time for making drawings of military fortifications. He also wrote his first letter to *The Times* about the disgraceful decay of the English monument at Albucra – and had the satisfaction of knowing by mid-November that it was being repaired.

Early in 1901 Shem went to Frankfurt where he was so cold that he slept with his feet in a big stove, and a man was found frozen to death in the street underneath his window. He was appointed Lector at Jena University in 1901, and also got private pupils, being paid two marks per hour. In June 1902 he had to have three bones removed from his right elbow. He had seen a surgeon in Berlin who wanted to amputate his arm, but he chose instead a surgeon called Riedel, who was surgeon to the Czar, and who operated on him in Jena. By then Shem had been befriended by the Ludwigs, Gertrude being headmistress of the Girls High School, and the most prolific writer of postcards the Moores ever encountered. Grandpa rushed over to be with him, and in July the first bandages were removed from his elbow, without an anaesthetic. In September, still weak, he came home.

In 1903 Shem began work as Modern Languages Master at the School for the Sons of Missionaries, at Blackheath. By now he was carrying out a considerable number of preaching engagements, once even preaching impromptu to two tramloads of people waiting to go back to London: 'trams with open tops had their advantages' he declared. He also went to hear debates in the House of Commons, but in October was back in St Thomas's Hospital for two weeks with another arm operation. The year was overshadowed by Uncle William Smith being drowned in Africa: 'My only great friend', wrote Shem.

1904 was more cheerful. At Easter the famous reading party took place when he took four women to Paris – my Auntie Gertie Moore, Aunt Ann Smith (my father's sister), 'Aunt' Marion Broadhead (the Macclesfield miniature artist) and Evelyn Kermode of Congleton. (The Kermodes were a large Wesleyan family whom my Father always referred to as the Commodes). In Paris Shem overheard someone say *'C'est un Turc: le violà avec ces quatre femmes!'* In August he rented a house in Welling, and he was married to Auntie Florence. The honeymoon was in Exeter, Bude and Boscastle, and even included going to tea with Marie Corelli. They had two sons; Will Greyburn Moore was born on 24th July 1905, and Hubert Prichard (Bun) three years later. Shem also added to his workload that of becoming a London County Council lecturer, his first course being given in Whitechapel on eighteenth century literature – this was a failure. But drama always surrounded him, even on going on a walk up Shooter's Hill with two-year-old Will. A weasel dashed out of a wood and began rushing madly round Shem's legs. He lifted Will shoulder-high as another came and joined in the circling. They only left when Shem stamped hard.

In 1911 he was Senior Modern Language Master at Eltham College, and in 1914 to the distress of many (including himself) he was not made headmaster. He had got his London BA, and was undertaking many preaching engagements, both in this country and in France. In 1914 he was appointed to Bishop Stortford School and filled any spare time with the cricket he so loved. In 1917 the school won the French President's Sèvres vase for its prowess in French – and Shem got his London MA.

On May 29th 1918 Shem was appointed headmaster of Silcoates

School, near Wakefield. To celebrate he brought a new drawing-room suite for £12. Silcoates was a small independent public school, founded in 1820, with entry then restricted to the sons of Congregational Ministers and Missionaries. Even after widening its intake to admit the sons of laymen, there were only fifty-six boys there. In 1904 a disastrous fire had destroyed all the buildings except the eighteenth century Silcoates Hall, which was the headmaster's house, and Shem's happy home for the next twenty-five years. Now it is a prosperous school with over five hundred pupils, and still renowned for its scholastic achievements.

Shem's reign at Silcoates made him a legend; in vacations he pioneered wonderful and exciting school trips all over Europe; he was an inspired language teacher, and the school for five years won the Sèvres vases for their achievements in French. He was himself awarded the decoration of *Officier d'Académie* by the French Government. He took boys to exhibitions in this country and he attracted to the school the famous and the interesting. He flew over Yorkshire with Sir Alan Cobham, he enlarged the school with a new Chapel and new buildings, and he continued to play his beloved cricket with one arm. He was always proud of the fact that the last game of cricket played by W.G. Grace was with himself in the long distant past.

All this took a toll of his health, which first began to show signs of strain when his younger son, Bun, died of pneumonia in 1924, aged sixteen years. At the end of that year Shem had a breakdown, resulting in six weeks in a nursing home, and then a holiday for six weeks in Bandol, with Auntie Florence. She was a wonderful wife, with a great sense of humour, and beloved of generations of schoolboys. Very lame, she became a hopeless invalid in her last years, but was incredibly brave. Often Shem, by the end of the school year, had become over-tired, and troubled by phlebitis and bronchitis. He used to retreat to Chamonix, in Switzerland, to recuperate, recharging his batteries by reading in the peace of the Alps. In 1939 he was made Chairman of the Yorkshire Congregational Union – a rare honour for one who was a Methodist. In 1942 he went back as preacher at Eltham College's centenary service, where an old pupil of his had been Fenner Brockway. Among Shem's friends were Dr Schwitzner, Pastor Niemoeller and Dr Nat Micklem. He devoted his retirement to writing books on German hymnology and articles on German poets. His love of English literature never abated; by the age of fifteen years his parents had encouraged him to read all Scott, all Dickens and nearly all Shakespeare, and this had laid the groundwork for an ever-increasing appreciation of the wealth that lay in books.

When Shem died in 1964 his successor at Silcoates School, himself an old boy, wrote in the school magazine: 'Take an electrifying personality, a mind richly stored and always wide open, vivid realism, genius for teaching, love and care for each individual in his community, stoutness of heart, natural leadership, incomparable panache and sense of occasion and you have just a few of the ingredients which made the legend and the reality.' Uncle Sydney always seemed larger than life, and even brief meetings left you breathless, primed with new ideas, and clutching a copy of a new author, snatched from his shelves, with the order that you must read it.

Unfortunately Shem was too ill to carry out his great wish, to catch the first train to Jena after the end of hostilities. After Auntie Florence died in 1951, he married Margaret Just, and lived happily and quietly with her at Letchworth, his life much enriched by visits from Will and his grandchildren. Margaret was a distant relation of the Spencer-Churchills, so Shem at once wrote to my mother 'How do you like being related to Winston?' As Winston was one of her heroes she was extremely pleased, but also we all loved Margaret for her gentleness and kindness.

Chapter Five

The Whistons and the Smales

Granny's two sisters 'married well'. Emma Smith Prichard, the eldest, (1847 – 1885) married William Whiston (1838 – 1915). He was the owner of Langley Silk Printworks and became a Justice of the Peace and an alderman of Cheshire County Council. He had inherited the business from his uncle, John Smith, who in turn had inherited it from William Smith, the founder. Uncle Whiston left £131,115 (£92,771 net) when he died in 1915, besides all the money he had settled on his children. He was known as a benevolent employer and as being kind to his wife's relations. Pure silk dress lengths were sent down to Wood Villa, so that his sister-in-law and nieces could choose what they wanted, and his carriage would meet the train in Macclesfield when Mother had been attending a late concert in Manchester, so that she did not have to walk the three miles home through lonely Langley Wood. Although she had been known as a tomboy, she could be very nervous, and often blessed the fact that hatpins were fashionable in her youth. They proved excellent defensive weapons as she discovered, especially during more than one journey to and from Manchester in a railway carriage that had no corridor!

Emma Whiston died in 1885, leaving her husband with nine children. In 1886 he married the children's governess, Louisa Milne, who made a kind and excellent stepmother. They had no children. My mother was devoted to Flo, the eldest Whiston daughter. I never knew her, but she was always glamorous to me as she had refused an offer of marriage from Stanley Baldwin before she married Tom Worth, who died a year after their wedding. She then married Arthur Simon. Cousin Edith Whiston, the next daughter, (1867 – 1947) I did know. She was thin and decisive and I was scared of her. I only warmed to her in 1929 when she stayed with us for two nights in Newcastle upon Tyne, on her way back to Macclesfield from Carnoustie Hydro where she had been on holiday. The main purpose of her visit to us was so that she could go and see the North East Coast Exhibition and she revealed quite a different side of her character to me. She insisted on taking me to see the Wall of Death, and we had a wonderful time, clutching one another at the guard rail and wondering if the roaring motor bike would dash over the top into us. I nearly ruined our new relationship, for Mother, flown with the success of the visit, told me to call our visitor 'Edith', and to drop the prefix 'Cousin'. I tried it at table and can still see Cousin Edith's look of revulsion. Mother explained it was her fault. In those days the young (I was thirteen) addressed their elders with formality which is why I am always so sorry for the elderly incarcerated in institutions who are called by their Christian names by the nurses and carers. Many of them hate it and come of the generation when we were not all equal and status was acquired by the respectability of marriage.

Cousin Mim Whiston was a Christian Scientist and had soft fluffy hair like a rabbit's. She had once planted a load of tulip bulbs all the wrong way up and Cousin Connie Smale had a low opinion of her intelligence. But I respected her. She drove a small car, and when I myself started driving she imparted to me the secret weapon with which she faced any mechanical problem. 'Now dear,' she said, 'if you break down, open the bonnet of the car, and stand over it with a large screwdriver in your hand. You will find help comes at once – no man can bear the thought of you damaging an engine.' I have not put it to the test yet but carry it in my head as a useful reserve trick, to be used if necessary.

Uncle Whiston's younger son, Cousin Hartington Whiston, who lived next door to Granny's at Invercraig, was the manager of the

Printworks and noted for his honesty and kindness. He had been a skilled musician. He and his wife had five children: Eric (to whom my mother had taught music), Sybil and Sheila, and then, much later, the twins, Elsa and Neil. Their garden had small ponds in a rockery, in which pink water lilies flowered, to my envy.

The real star of the Whiston family, in my youth, was cousin Harold, William Whiston's oldest son (1873 – 1952), who had inherited Langley Print Works from his father in 1915. He was a self-satisfied man whose empire gradually disintegrated. It was not all his fault of course, for national and international economic stresses affected the fortunes of the silk industry between the wars. It was common gossip however that he wasted a lot of money through importing German scientists to further his dream of making pure cloth of gold. He bought Sutton Grange to live in ('Ten gardeners and a private aerodrome!' hissed Auntie Gertie, her eyes popping with excitement). When I was sixteen years old I remember meeting him, just after he had come back from a business trip to Turkey. He described to me a visit he had been taken on to see the inmates of a harem. 'They are all,' he assured me seriously, 'recognised by their smells.' I repeated this innocently to Daddy who nearly had hysterics. Cousin Harold brought much colour into our family life, but he was kind and especially so to Granny. He installed, at different times, the first flush lavatory she had: it was just outside the back door, with a covered porch. Later he had Uncle Sydney's old back bedroom at Wood Villa made into a bathroom. (Very nice until one year Auntie Gertie, much given to doing hasty make do and mend in the house decided the bath needed repainting. No number of fresh coats and no amount of expert inspections ever brought the surface back to a comfortable smoothness). I think, too, Cousin Harold installed the electricity in the house. Soon afterwards I saw Grandpa, exasperated by not being able to pull the plug of an electric fire out of its socket, get his penknife out and insert it in the side of the plug. It shot up and hit the ceiling, narrowly missing him. 'Really, Father,' said Mother, 'You might have been killed.' Granny would never say anything unkind about Cousin Harold, though she pulled some mysterious faces at times; but then she always tried to find the good in people. A relative said that he had been 'spoilt by adulation from birth, and self-centredness', but acknowledged he was kind.

My chief association with the Whistons was that every summer Mother and Granny took me to tea at Clough House, clad in my Sunday hat, coat, frock and gloves. It was an exciting house, much extended to fit the large Whiston family. On the left of the front door was the dining-room, with the smoking-room behind. On the right of the hall was the Library, full of leather-bound volumes in pristine condition: one walked through it to the big drawing-room which had a great beautifully carved Chinese cabinet in it that Uncle Whiston had brought back from China. French doors led into the conservatory with its sweet smelling heliotrope or 'cherry pie', and its glass cases of shells and fossilised sea creatures, including seahorse skeletons (which I particularly coveted). Off the conservatory was the Games Room, where Cousin Mim sportingly played puff ball and bagatelle with nieces and nephews. The last room was the Billiard Room, with its gloomy suits of armour standing round the shrouded billiard table.

A lot of the overseas furniture (including the three huge iron storks at the bottom of the lawn) was from Uncle Whiston's travels. He allowed each of his nine children a country to visit when they became twenty-one years old, and he and Auntie Whiston went there as well, bringing back all sorts of trophies. Cousin Mim had certainly displayed great intelligence on the occasion when she chose her trip – she wanted to go round the world, so this is what they did!

I was terrified when I went there to tea, in case I made a social gaffe. The bread and butter was transparent, but the porcelain tea service was even thinner and was positively unnerving. I was always sure I would one day bite the edge of my cup and snap a piece off. Luckily I never did, though my teeth always rattled nervously on the rim of the cup.

Sometimes when we stayed at Wood Villa kind Auntie Whiston would send her car to take Granny, Mother and me into town to shop.

A great treat, especially as I discovered to my pride that my mother knew how and when and what to tip the chauffeur. When Auntie Gertie was old and nearly all the Whistons were dead, I was shocked to hear her suddenly burst out about how she had hated receiving their many kindnesses, and how she had resented always being 'the poor relation'. Apparently she took much pride in later years in telling Edith and Mim that my parents would that day be having lunch with the Duke of Devonshire! It had never occurred to me before that she had these feelings, and I wondered how she reconciled them with her deep religious convictions.

Village life was of course centred on the Printworks, which was the main employer of the neighbourhood, and even attracted a workforce that walked up from Macclesfield daily. I once remember waking in pitch blackness, when I still slept in my parents' bedroom, and being frightened by a tremendous noise outside on the road. It was very early in the morning, and the sound was that of people going past the house, all wearing clogs on their feet; they were on their way to the Printworks.

The Smales

Granny's younger sister, Louisa Adeline Prichard (1854 – 1926) married William Smale and lived at Field Bank, Oxford Road, Macclesfield. It was a large detached house, standing on a little hillock in spacious grounds – at one time a little girl called Vera Brittain used to toddle through the hedge from next door to watch the tennis, and my mother had to take her back home. Money and servants abounded: at Field Bank my mother's cross was to go there to the Christmas Party for, when the trifle was served, Grandpa invariably asked, 'Is there any of the demon drink in this, Louisa?' Auntie Louie assured him there was not (though I gathered from Mother that it was well laced) the maids would snigger and Mother would nearly die of shame.

37

Auntie Louie was generous and had all the Prichard kindness. She needed it, for her husband's memory became blurred and left him comparatively early in life, so he always had a male attendant with him both indoors and out. They had three daughters, Constance (my Aunt Connie, 1876 – 1965), Ada (1878 – 1965) and Kate Lisette (1881 – 1964). They were all educated at Cheltenham Ladies' College, at least one of them becoming head girl. Aunt Connie looked like a parrot: she had almost married a Portuguese grandee and was a tremendous sport, with a great sense of humour. Auntie Ada had a lot of ill health and worked for the blind, and the youngest, Aunt Kittie, married Colonel Noah Heath, and she too had three daughters, Thelma, Joyce and Norah. They were charming girls full of sport and fun, and I remember them calling at Granny's on their way back from a ride in the hills. Thelma was on her father's powerful and prancing big hunter which he had expressly forbidden her to ride: the groom was in a terrible state about it, and confided to us he expected to be sacked when they got home. Joyce was on Thelma's horse, and Norah on another. They were all keen on hunting and Thelma, after turning down numerous offers of marriage, met and married the Master of the Devon Foxhounds. Norah married a Master of Staghounds.

Aunt Kittie was kind – at a time when my pocket money was 4d per week she once tipped me 5/-, to my intense joy. All the Smales gave me lovely presents, with the exception of one unfortunate gift from Aunt Connie. I was ill in bed at Wood Villa with tonsillitis, and she sent me up a book about a zebra that lost its mummy. Daddy started to read it aloud to me but I sobbed so loud and long that he had to stop. All the family read it and kept assuring me it did find its mummy in the end, but I did not believe them. I still have the book and have never read it.

Uncle Noah was kind too – he would often drop a brace of pheasant or partridge off at Granny's when he was riding home after hunting. (Auntie Gertie loved rushing them into the cellar to hang until they were high enough to cook, thereby ruining them for most of us.) At Granny's funeral he was deeply moved – they had had a loving aunt-nephew relationship for many years. I think each realised and appreciated the inherent goodness in each other. Uncle Noah was an outstanding man, and as Deputy Lord Lieutenant of Cheshire did a lot of good.

Chapter Six

Evelyn Prichard Smith, née Moore

My mother, Evelyn Prichard (1886 – 1967), was brought up strictly – Chapel four times on Sundays, and Grandpa would not allow story books to be read, nor dolls to be played with, on the Sabbath. Indeed, Mother never got to a theatre until after she was married at the age of twenty-seven years. In spite of the moral and physical harshness of life at Langley, where in winter you broke the ice each morning on top of the ewer in your bedroom, Mother led a happy life, and some of the photographs of her show her as something of a tomboy. She was a frequent visitor to favourite cousins at Ellenhall and Nantwich, where they made cowslip balls in the fields and played games. Auntie Gertie, her senior by twelve years, and Uncle Sydney, older by eight years, often had their friends staying at Wood Villa. My grandparents there also kept open house – Methodist ministers abounded. Family friends included the Broadheads of Manchester whose daughter, Marian Ellen, was about Auntie Gertie's age, and her contemporary at the Girls' High School. 'Auntie' Marian became a famous miniature painter, and the Moores were good subjects to paint: some of the miniatures were hung in the Royal Academy. So there was a steady stream of visitors coming to the house, and return visits were made to surrounding homesteads.

Uncle Sydney's great friendship with William (Will) Smith of Buxton Road, Macclesfield, dated back to 1895, and meant all the Smith family formed strong links with the life of the Moores back at Wood

Villa. After Uncle Sydney married Florence Gibson of Bridlington this opened up yet another area to explore with new friends to meet. Then he moved to Welling and Granny, Auntie Gertie and Mother were frequent visitors there, looking after babies and going to improving lectures in London. He was very good at taking his sisters to interesting events and even, on 5 February 1910, took my Mother as his partner (Florence being ill) to a grand dinner at the Café Royal, Regent Street. This was run by the *Societé Nationale des Professeurs de Français en Angleterre,* in honour of the French Ambassador, M. Paul Cambon. Never had mother been to a nine course dinner before, which cost nine and sixpence per head! She never forgot the glory of the occasion.

Grandpa, of course, was all over the country, selling chairs, and sending postcards home giving news of his whereabouts, and of orders he had taken. Occasionally Granny would go and stay at a lodging house in Blackpool, taking with her either Gertie or my Mother, both of whom succumbed to illness at times. Quinseys, influenza and fainting fits seemed to be the most popular ailments. Sometimes the two girls went alone to the same trusted lodging house, while the almost daily postcards shuttled to and from the family at Wood Villa, commenting on weather, dirty washing, money and village news. Correspondence loomed large in those pre-telephone days, the more exotic items coming from Whistons and Smales, who roamed all over Europe in search of recuperation after any illness. But the most prolific postcard sender of all was Gertrude Ludwig of Jena who sent a ceaseless stream of cards to all the Moores, mostly written in German. Uncle Sydney, that great linguist, revelled in these, and as my Mother's German was quite good, they were also enjoyed by her.

Pictures of Mother show an attractive girl, with animated eyes, and tumbling curly black hair. She had Granny's gift of forming a trusting relationship with animals – especially cats, who followed her with adoring eyes. Floss, her ginger and much-loved cat at Langley, so loved Mother that when the latter was in bed for several months in 1906 with a tubercular ankle, Floss used to go off hunting in Langley

Wood, often bringing home a small rabbit that she would tenderly deposit on the invalid's bed. Floss had her miniature painted by Auntie Marian, and it still rests in the small golden locket, set with pearls and turquoises, where Mother had it put.

I have eight of Mother's school reports from Macclesfield Girls' High School. She went there at the age of eight years, but seems to have consistently been low in class, although the mistresses sometimes included encouraging remarks. Her needlework was very poor (and remained so all her life) but she was good at knitting. In spite of all this, in 1903, at the age of seventeen, she passed the University of Oxford Junior Local Examination in ten subjects. Her music was 'promising' at age twelve, but dropped back to 'fairly good' at age fourteen years. However, at age thirteen, in 1899, she had got her certificate for elementary pianoforte playing from the Incorporated Society of Music, and then her Grade 3 certificate in 1901.

In 1902 she was awarded a First Class certificate (Senior section) of the London College of Music, and passed the Local Practical Examination in Grade 4 (Advanced) of the Incorporated Society of Musicians in 1904. In 1907 she got a pass certificate from the Associated Board of the Royal Academy of Music, and also a certificate for the advanced grade.

Mother became a student at the Royal Manchester College of Music, Ducie Street, Manchester in 1907, having won a Cheshire County Scholarship there for four years. She studied piano under Egon Petri, who had been a pupil of Busoni's and was the foremost interpreter of that great pianist's compositions. Petri had been encouraged to devote himself to the piano by Paderewski, and was acclaimed as one of the greatest players of Beethoven, Bach and Liszt. Neville Cardus said Petri brought Beethoven to the Islington Hall at Ancoats 'like a living presence'. He made 'a rare contribution to Manchester music' in his six years there. Carl Fuchs referred to him as 'a great pianist'. He was an international figure: after Manchester he taught in Berlin and at Basle (where he had as a pupil John Ogden) and after 1939 he worked in America. Mother adored him, although he wrote about her work in 1910: 'Is no doubt very gifted both musically and technically, but is rather disappointing by never attaining to perfection in her performances. After all, correctness is essential, though not everything.' I only met him once, on 24th January 1939, when he played in Leeds Town Hall, and the audience was entranced with his superb interpretation at the keyboard. After the concert he and Mrs Petri fell on Mother with joyful shouts of 'Evelyn!'

Mother studied harmony and composition under Dr Walter Carroll, who became a close friend of hers. His many letters to Mother reveal his anxiety about her health, for she was having trouble with her ankle. He gave her an excellent reference, saying in 1911, she 'is well qualified to teach pianoforte playing and rudiments of Music and Harmony'. Mother revelled in the life at the RMCM. The Principal was Dr. Adolph Brodsky, and on several Saturday afternoons in the year his quartet played in Manchester. Neville Cardus waxed lyrical about these concerts, saying of Brodsky 'his violin seemed to receive the music, not to play it.' Mother was there of course, and at the Hallé Society's concerts, conducted by Dr. Hans Richter – this was the golden age of music, and helping it along was Sammy Langford, the great SL, Music Critic of the *Manchester Guardian*. Cardus venerated SL and wrote in his autobiography 'the greatest man I have ever known'. Cardus also used to go to the Students' Musical Evenings: I wonder if he was there on 16th March 1909, when Mother played two Ballads of Brahms?

Mother also took part in local concerts: In October 1906 she played Love Song (Hensett) and Toccata (Macfarren) in the Mechanic's Institute, Hazel Grove, and in 1909 Liszt's Rhapsodie at Longsight Wesleyan Circuit's Literary and Musical Evening (admission 6d). In 1910 Macclesfield Drill Hall held a concert in aid of the Boy Scouts at which she played Liszt (Concert Study in D Flat and Rhapsody XII). The press notice said this was highly appreciated, though the Zither Banjo selections were 'splendid' and, one suspected, stole the limelight. Langley Choral Society's concert in 1911 had Mother playing Liszt's twelfth Rhapsody, while her cousin Hartington Whiston (Baritone) sang Mandalay (Front seats one shilling). The Choral Society held a Grand Coronation Concert on 26 April 1911 in the presence of His Worship the Mayor of Macclesfield. Mother was by now an Associate of the Royal Manchester College of Music, and played Chopin's Ballade in A Flat, while Cousin Hartington sang 'Gentlemen – the King!'. Auntie Gertie was billed among the trebles, and as mother was pianist for the whole evening, the family played a full part in the proceedings. This carried on a family tradition, for Granny was an excellent pianist too, and in much demand, both locally and in Macclesfield.

During all this musical furore, whilst Mother was emerging as a concert pianist and teacher of music, her private life was being enriched too. My father was courting her. Their engagement was recorded by Granny writing to her son, Sydney, in an undated letter, but believed to be in 1907:

'My own "real" boy, forgive me not writing sooner, this love affair has been such a thunderbolt to me. I seem quite vacant or something. On Friday night Daddy came in and said I overtook two people by Foden Bank and it was Eve and Frank – he was pushing the bike and Eve had his arm. Pa said, "Oh it's you two is it?" Frank said, "I was coming to see you tonight, Mr Moore, on an important event, I want you to let me have Evelyn." I don't know what else was said, but Eve said, "Well, you do like Frank, Daddy, don't you?" He said, "I'll go on and tell Mother." He came in and I nearly shook, Frank came and said could he speak to me, we went in the Drawing Room and had a chat, then Eve came in and I said, "Frank wants my baby." "Well, Mother, you will gain a son," she replied. I kissed them both but said nothing much, only that Eve would have no fortune, I might give her a few pounds, but he didn't seem to mind that, but there is no one whom I would rather have Evelyn, Frank is very good, a real Christian, and he has

45

come along and tried to fill that "big gap" caused by "our other boy" being taken "Home" so early, had he been spared Frank would have had a poor chance with Eve, I believe. Well, I dare not have refused Frank, for somehow I've always felt Eve so safe when he has been taking her anywhere. I hope it's all for the best. I am not looking at this time for her leaving us, that is too premature, she is hot in love and so is Frank, their faces do beam. Daddy seems very glad, and says there is no one he would rather have than Frank, but it's a big shock to me, and you should hear Gertie giving them some sound advice. She told them if she had been at home "this" would never have happened....She will have a lot to learn before she is fit to be a wife, dear child. I told Frank I did not like the thought of her going to Church as I was a Methodist to my backbone, he said he should go to *her* "place of worship".... I woke yesterday morning to feel Daddy laughing, I said, "What is the matter?" He said, "I was thinking about Eve saying, you do like Frank don't you?" Your father has had a bit of fun of this saying, and will tell you when he sees you again.'

Mother was also spreading her wings, and went for a holiday with the C.H.A. to Boscastle, Cornwall, in the summer of 1910. Father was there, as her fiancé, and she wrote back to Granny 'Frank is good to me. He looks after me like a mother! He's a dear good boy.'

One trip was to Clovelly – 'It's a thirty mile drive each way – sixty altogether. We reckon to get to Clovelly in three hours with two fresh relays of horses on the way.' Another letter said 'Have had a long drive to Pentire Head. On the return drive we'd four horses to our charabanc and we did fly!' They suffered agonies with sunburn, and Mother, very thirsty on the journey, unwisely drank some cider at one stop, not realising how potent it was. My parents both loved Boscastle, and went there again after they were married, acting as host and hostess to the C.H.A. house party. They took me to see the place one afternoon in the 1930s. Later my description of the great storm that was blowing during my visit, with the waves crashing all over the place, was judged the best holiday essay in my class at school.

My father finally got a lectureship at the College at Aberystwyth, and for reasons I have never really understood, he and my Mother got married very quietly on 31st December 1913, without telling my grandmother, although my grandfather was present. Granny, much as she liked Father, could not bear the thought of losing her youngest daughter, and was apt to dissolve in tears at the thought, so they felt it would be kinder to present her with a *fait accompli.* 'Everyone thought I must be pregnant,' said Mother many years later, 'but of course I wasn't.' Granny, once she got over the shock, took it very well. Neither family had any money, and this may well have been the major consideration in the plan. My parents went to Shanklin in the Isle of Wight for their honeymoon, after a few days in London. 'Frank is a darling and giving me a gorgeous holiday, I might be a princess by the way he looks after me,' wrote Mother enthusiastically to her home. 'My purple hat suits me beautifully. Frank is charmed with it.' This last sentence is very funny, for my father never had any interest in clothes and shopping, but love's young dream evidently cast a glow over his usual approach to the subject.

Mother enjoyed her role as a University bride. Other staff wives urged her to use their piano until hers arrived, formalities of paying calls and of leaving visiting cards were explored, family and friends came to stay, all delighting in the natural beauty of Cardigan Bay, and long exploratory walks were taken. On 10th September 1914 my sister, Gwyneth Prichard Smith, was born and Mother's cup was full. Eight months later Gwyneth died of bronchial pneumonia, and my parents' world crashed. Mother was inconsolable. They took the tiny body back to the family vault at St James Church, a mile from Langley. Later Mother wrote to Granny that 'the house was so quiet now'. I was not born until 7th November 1916, and Mother became fiercely possessive, scarcely letting me out of her sight for years. I never fought this, for it was based on such total love and dedication, but it lasted until I was grown up. I can well remember my inner terror when I was a Social Studies student at Leeds University, and went to my first practical placement, where I was told I would visit clients in their own homes. I was sure Mummy would not let me trot alone round the slums of Leeds, but to my surprise she took it quite calmly. I simply announced over the luncheon table that I was going to do home visits, and wasn't it exciting! In 1945 I had another inward tussle, when the old feeling of guilt loomed up in me. Granny had left me £25, and it was in the bank. I was out for supper and another social worker who was present said she would sell her car to anyone for £20 – it had just been squashed flat by an Army lorry, but the insurance company was repairing it. I said quickly 'I'll give you £25', and found I had bought a 1938 Austin 8. I then remembered Mother had expressly forbidden me ever to get a car. I dared not tell her. Eventually I admitted it to my father, and I heard him saying in an amazed voice to Mother, 'She's bought a car!' My terror subsided: her only proviso was that I should have some proper lessons. In the event it was a masterly stroke, for in the last two years in Leeds I was able to collect Father off the London train, late at night and, as he became more frail, drive them everywhere. He was charmed with the way I could park in town in about a couple of feet, whereas his 20 horsepower Armstrong Siddeley took up the space of two ordinary cars. I drove 119,000 miles and then sold it for £95 – 'the only smart deal this family has ever done,' said my Father approvingly, as he watched me bolt out of the house to put the cheque in the bank. It was a superb car: nothing locked, and it had a soft top that concertinaed down which, as Mother pointed out, allowed us three large Smiths room to expand upwards, if not sideways. If one lost the ignition key, a paper clip was a perfectly adequate substitute. Ah, those were the days!

In later years, Mother nursed my Father devotedly, but after his death in 1951 she always looked lost – to the end they had remained deeply in love. Her rheumatism increased with old age, and for the last seven years of her life she was practically housebound. One consolation was the advent of Mahitabel, a stray tom cat who arrived starving at our house in a blizzard, and who speedily reduced Mother and me to slavery. He was a black and white alley cat of great character, always anxious to please. He was not house trained, and misbehaved the first night. Mother gave him a strict talking to, so he never again misbehaved for the last ten years of his life. The fishman called daily with two slices of cod for him ('Mrs Smith must be ill', said a neighbour to our doctor, 'I see the fishman calling every day.') Mahitabel would lie motionless on the lawn in the sun, while a mother thrush would parade her two babies round him, after Mummy had explained to him he was not to touch them. He had admirers all over the world who sent him Christmas cards.

Mother was heartbroken when Mahitabel died, and I at once got her a television set which she had always said we could not afford. Luckily, tennis at Wimbledon was on, and she enjoyed it tremendously. She was always thrilled when someone came on she knew, such as Leslie Sands, the actor, whom we had known well in Leeds.

She was in constant pain, and it got worse. In 1967 her legs refused to work one evening. A gerontologist came, and she was admitted to hospital for treatment, but she deteriorated, and I drove home from hospital twice a day with my face nearly blinded with tears. I had said that if she was dying she was to come home, so after fourteen days she came back to me in a coma, to sleep away in my arms seventeen hours later. By God's grace she knew she was home: I had called to her inanimate figure for three hours saying, 'Mummy darling, you're home and safe with me.' Suddenly she pulled herself up in the bed and bowed to me – she could not speak, and sank back into unconsciousness. She had always said hospital would kill her, but she went in willingly, knowing I could not lift and nurse her.

Friends said we were more like sisters than Mother and daughter. She was an ageless companion, brilliant and full of fun and flashes of loving inspiration. Together the three of us, Father, Mother and I had been all in all to each other, enjoying life to the full. Now I was on my own.

Chapter Seven

The Smiths

My father, Frank Smith (1882 – 1951) had a complex and colourful background. He was born at 74, Brook Street, Macclesfield, and within the year his father, a coach decorator called Matthew Smith (1843 – 1883), the son of a hatter, John Smith of Nixon's Yard, died of diabetes. Matthew left his wife, Alice (1844 – 1918) with seven children, the oldest being a boy of fourteen years. Grandma Alice Smith was not daunted by her task, and displayed vigour and kindly efficiency in carrying out her role as housemaker. She never ran into debt, although her income was £200 per annum: out of it she even managed to take all the children away every summer for a ten day seaside holiday – a rare treat for a poor family in those days.

Grandma Alice was from Worsley, and was the daughter of Edmund and Lizzie Simister, who sold potatoes at a stall in Shude Hill Market, Manchester. She owned some cottage property which was let at rents ranging from 1/8d per week (one up and one down type) up to 5/- per week for a three bedroomed house. When all the tenants paid their rents it brought in an income of just over £2 per week. In addition Grandma Alice Smith had the largest share in some other property, including shops and a farm, which the family always grandiloquently referred to as 'the estate'. The income from this was divided every quarter with various relatives. It was Grandma Alice Smith's job to manage the 'estate' and keep the books. Through family changes the shares were reckoned by a complicated method, so that Grandma

51

Alice's own share was one fifth, one half of one fifth, and one fifth of one fifth. Each quarter the recipients mustered at the Smith's house in Nixon's Yard for the share out, headed by the next most important shareholder, an Aunt Lizzie who was the widow of Matthew Smith's brother Thomas. She was only entitled to one fifth, and one half of one fifth, but not to one fifth of one fifth as well. She never understood this point and bitterly resented it: at every quarterly gathering her aggressive bonnet and set face announced she wanted her right. She also fought the cost of repairs to the property, and even seemed to think Grandma Alice Smith responsible for any increase in local authority rates.

Although this Aunt Lizzie originally came from Birmingham, Thomas Smith had met her in Australia in the gold rush – how she got there is obscure. She married him because he was the only prospector she met who said he was returning to England. She was a business woman to her fingertips, but she could only write her name, and taught herself to read. She was an exquisite needlewoman, and earned a living by making fine collars for parsons. She ruled her six children with a rod of iron and a harshness that was in violent contrast to Grandma Smith's gentler methods. One of the few people who could handle her was my Father, who I think enjoyed her strange use of language and unique pronunciation 'Which omitted every legitimate aspirate and added one to every word that began with a vowel.'

But Father's most original relative was Thomas Lowe, the widower of Matthew Smith's sister, Eliza. He had a streak of genius that the family thought was akin to insanity. By his first marriage to Eliza he had five children, who inherited some of their father's eccentricity. He was an advertising agent and bill poster, a man of great ostentation and show. He drove about in a trap drawn by a spirited pony, going at a reckless gallop over the countryside to announce some forthcoming agricultural show, or travelling circus. He was also an agent for Sanger's Circus, and once persuaded them to spend the winter in Macclesfield: his five children and my Father's elder brothers all had free passes for admission. My Father was judged too young to savour these delights, but I well remember his stories of how he used to crawl under the canvas into the big top. Thomas Lowe's second marriage was to a headmistress from Cornwall, the sister of a local mayor. He only told her he had one boy – the first of many shocks when she met the rest of the children. Her family never forgave her for marrying him. Grandma Alice Smith went to see her one day in her Macclesfield home and found her frying chops wearing her best gloves – she was completely undomesticated. For many years she was 'too grand' to know my Father's family.

It was Thomas Lowe's two elder daughters who brought romance and colour into my Father's life. Martha Ann, born 1882, accompanied by her sister Emily, went to America: at the age of twenty-one years they had each inherited a small sum of money from a relative, and Emily's young man (whom she eventually did not marry) was out there. On the boat Martha Ann met a German who was being shipped out and 'got rid of' by his family. The story was that the captain of the ship 'got them married', the new husband spent all Martha Ann's money, and they then went back to Germany. She never learnt German, and never settled. When my Father was about eight years old she burst back into the Smith lives, full of stories of religious feuds and of hostile relatives who sought her life. She dramatised herself as a new Joan of Arc, and fascinated my Father. Five years later she came over to England again, displaying cut hands which she said were caused by escaping from her house. She refused to return to Germany, saying her husband was a party in a plot to kill her. She stayed with the Smiths for some months, eventually running round the house with a carving knife. She was then sent to Parkside Asylum in Macclesfield, and died there in 1962, my Father's sisters, Auntie Annie and Auntie Edie visiting her there faithfully until she died.

Cousin Hannah was another of Thomas Lowe's daughters and was born in 1856. She never married, although as she herself often said, she had all the world at her feet. She was less eccentric than her sister Martha Ann. She was a nurse, first at an asylum near Manchester, and then a sister in a London asylum. She lived in Acton, and her visits back to Macclesfield were spectacular. Father, as a boy, thought the way she dressed and talked aristocratic. Tall, handsome and adorned in star-spangled ornaments and jewellery, with a gay laugh and lively wit, she shed on his provincial home something of the brilliance of high society. She had, or so it seemed, been everywhere and knew everybody. She had an intimate knowledge of the Royal family, a profound respect for Queen Victoria, and made mischievous references to a prince she called 'Teddy'. On her days off at the hospital she 'dressed to kill' and scoured the West End, where she knew everyone by sight. She got to know servants at the big houses, and so got all the gossip. It was suspected by the Smiths that she had men friends: she certainly went on holiday to Scotland with a Rates Collector, Harry Dranfield, whom she later refused to marry when his wife died, because she would then lose her pension. Her social impact on the conforming and respectable Smith family had to be experienced to be believed, and her extravagant stories were mulled over for years, with many a chuckle.

Grandma Alice Smith's youngest sister, my Father's Aunt Tizzie, also deserves mention. She and her husband kept a public house not far from Brook Street, in a poor district of Macclesfield. At a time when drunkenness was common and ale was a penny a glass, a public house was open from early morning until 11 p.m. (10 p.m. on Sundays) and my father had the run of the place as a boy. He was often used to convey home some semi-helpless drunk, and his experiences with them gave him a deep hatred of drink. I never saw him drink beer, though he enjoyed a glass of wine when out at dinner parties. He never forbade me to drink, and we always had sherry and wine served at the dinners we gave ourselves. I only once saw him briefly the worse for wear, after Cousin Molly Moore at Ellenhall made him try a small glassful of her homemade cowslip wine. We drove away from her house in a series of figure eights up the road, but he soon pulled himself together.

Aunt Tizzie's daughter, Agnes Bell, became a clerical officer in Manchester, but returned to Macclesfield and took over the running of the Post Office at Rainow, living in a Smith cottage at Tower Hill. She was very proud of the fact that she was the first girl in Macclesfield to ride a bicycle, and her photo shows her standing by it. She never married, but towards the end of her life she told me everyone had expected her to marry my Father because as children she could make him do anything she wanted. She then added 'But I could never have been the hostess for him that your mother was'. I refrained from telling her of the depth of his affection for my Mother that persisted all through their marriage.

My Father's oldest brother, John (1868 – 1946) was witty and amusing, a good mimic and sought after singer of comic songs. However, he turned away from any difficulty and was carefree, delighting in the admiration he found in clubs and pubs. He drifted from one job to another, starting as an Apothecary's assistant, and then he became a coal man, the coal coming in barges to Macclesfield. All his jobs were doomed to failure through his careless neglect, for he had no sense of responsibility. One wonders now if his Father's death when he was an adolescent had a disastrous effect on him. In later years he lived with a succession of cousins, his brothers and sisters contributing a modest sum to pay for his keep. I only saw him once – a natty figure, in a well-brushed bowler hat, prancing into his sister's house in Buxton Road.

Two of Father's sisters, Ann (1873 -1963) and Edith (1880 – 1971) became pupil teachers, the latter completing her training at Whitelands College. They worked as teachers all their lives in Macclesfield. They were the core of the Smith family that I knew, for Father's mother, Grandma Alice Smith, had died when I was aged one year and three-quarters. I can just remember being put on the garden seat in 1918 at 'Tresmeer', Buxton Road, where the Smiths had moved to in 1905, while Father went into the house to see her for the last time. He was devoted to his mother, for they had helped one another all their lives, and he was extremely distressed by his visit. He records how he learned from her how to discern real need, fairness in the care of property, and how to give a stamped receipt, issue a rent book and keep a ledger, besides penning clear factual letters to disgruntled tenants. This indeed was one of his main sources of education.

I have always been puzzled by this early memory of mine, for I was so very young. Yet that visit is clear in my mind's eye, and I am quite sure I have not imagined it. I was heartened when recently re-reading Compton MacKenzie's *My Life and Times, Octave One*, by seeing that he insists he can recall quite clearly an event in his life that took place when he was only seven months old: he gives details of this memory, so my length of recall is not in the least impossible. Indeed he also claims continuous memory from before he was two years old.

Aunt Anne was sharp-tongued and kindly, with a lively wit. She was very pretty as a young girl and much teased about her matrimonial chances – my father addressed her as 'The Charmer'. Her siblings all wanted her to marry a local worthy, called George Henry Fletcher, but it never materialised. She thought he was mean, and great astonishment prevailed when my father once took me to see him when I was a little girl, and he presented me with sixpence – unheard of wealth. The next year I persuaded Daddy to take me to see George Henry again, but I got nothing. 'I told you so,' said Aunt Ann with a sniff. It was George Henry who chaired the 'Complimentary Social' that Macclesfield YMCA held in honour of my father when he left Macclesfield on 3rd September 1907.

Aunt Edie was large and slow, a great lover of literature and, in particular, of the Brontës. She was very artistic and attended embroidery classes after she retired, and also Heraldry classes. Her twin brother, George, first farmed and then became a rating officer, with a great love for, and knowledge of, Cheshire history. Another sister, Aunt Vinnie, had lived with Aunties Annie and Edie until her uncomplaining death in 1945 saddened us all. She was the domesticated one, peering through her pebble-thick glasses with her sweet and welcoming smile, and making the home one of comfort and solace for all. The three sisters shared a dislike of anyone whom they suspected of putting on airs, and roundly condemned some of my Mother's family for this suspected sin.

Aunt Annie always wanted to retire to a country house of charm, so after her retirement from teaching she and Aunt Edie used to go and inspect houses for sale all over the place. It became a mission in life, but we never thought they would leave 285 Buxton Road. However when Aunt Annie was over 90 years of age they took the plunge, building two extra bedrooms, sitting-room and boxroom on to Uncle George's cottage at Tower Hill, Rainow. He had moved there after his wife had died, and it was a charming establishment which they all enjoyed.

Aunts Ann and Edith both had an adventurous streak and had some wonderful holidays. Aunt Ann was one of the members of Uncle Sydney's Reading Party in Paris. Many years later the Aunts ventured across the English Channel again, by the shortest route possible, as they were prone to sea-sickness. On boarding the ship they at once went to their cabin. There they divested themselves of their clothing in order to plaster on their tummies sheets of brown paper well soaked in whisky, Aunt Ann having read in a magazine that this was a sure way to prevent sea-sickness. They were both strict teetotallers, and they reeked of whisky for days afterwards: the scheme was a failure in other ways too.

But the whole family had a sense of fun – as a young man Father had hired a horse and trap and took them to Buxton for the day. He had never driven before, and the horse bolted on the Cat and Fiddle moors. Until she died Aunt Edie talked of the terror during that ride.

The Aunts belonged to a strict mission church, at one time nearly becoming Plymouth Brethren. They never in their lives went to the cinema or theatre, but a friend lent them a television set in 1955, so that they could watch the Coronation. Aunt Ann (she always had histrionic leanings) could scarcely bear to turn it off, and indeed seemed to develop a great weakness for a dancing troupe called The Television Toppers, whom she condemned verbally, but watched on every occasion.

The most outstanding member of the family was the second boy, William (1877 – 1903), five years my Father's senior. He embodied all the qualities the Smiths most admired – a clear mind, and strong purpose, intelligence and unselfishness. He had made up his mind from an early age to be a schoolmaster. An avid reader who possessed great critical discernment, he attended University Extension Courses and then became a pupil teacher. Sitting the examination for this, in a school in Duke Street, Macclesfield, he sat next to the young man who became his greatest friend, my Uncle Sydney Moore.

Uncle Will's headmaster expected him to proceed to a training college for teachers after passing the Queen's Scholarship Examination. He had other plans: he knew Manchester University could be entered by means of the same examination. He passed First Class in the examination and in the next four years, at Owen's College, Manchester University, he received two degrees, MA and B.Sc., won an open University scholarship and was awarded many prizes. He was then employed as a teacher for three years, at Hanley and Bootle, and then went out to Klerksdorp in the Transvaal on a Government appointment as one of the twelve experts sent out to organise elementary and secondary education in the Transvaal. While swimming in a river on 30th October 1903 he was seized with cramp and drowned. This tragedy shattered the Smiths for a time, and Uncle Sydney revered his memory for the rest of his own long life. It had been expected by some that Will would marry my Mother eventually, though I do not think he was ever really in the running. He was close to all the Moores, and they shared to the full the grief that followed his death. The University obituary called him 'A man of the highest promise; he was respected by all who knew him.'

Chapter Eight

Frank Smith

The only school Father attended in this country was a Church Day School, and he left it at the age of thirteen years. He was there during the last years of the infamous system of payment by results, whereby the annual grants of the school were determined by an examination of the pupils, especially in the 'three Rs'. It was a good school of its kind, better than many of its rivals, for the Headmaster was an honest man, vigorous and efficient, and hating meanness and dishonesty. Initially Father was in the babies' class, perched on a gallery, peering down with between fifty and sixty other infants at a teacher who tried to teach them their letters. Later he was taught to memorise lists of prepositions, conjunctions and pronouns, and I have seen audiences convulsed with laughter when, fifty years later, he could reel them off in an apparently endless flow.

Father had no wish to become a teacher like Will, Ann and Edith, whom he saw enveloped in homework. He rejoiced in freedom. Yet at the age of twenty-four he was a university graduate, and at twenty-eight years back in the university doing post-graduate research: by his early forties he was occupying his first university chair. As a boy play had occupied most of his time, for playmates abounded, streets were safe, and he broadened his education by being in and out of a local joiner's shop, a builder's yard, a local bakehouse, a smithy and piggery. Silk weaving was still carried on in the garrets of the weavers' cottages. Street games in the neighbourhood helped to train all the youth of the area in planning how to enlarge and vary their skills, and indeed pioneered the 'projects' methods of the modern school. The latter are often the teacher's invention, kept going by his intervention, whereas Father discovered that a good project was one that found the answer to a problem that he or his friends discovered, and which was a challenge. Rivalry for leadership of the group was keen too, and this meant Father could lose any sense of inferiority he might have had in the home, where he was the youngest. I suspect he was a leader in many daring adventures during those formative years (I used to hear stories of raids on apple orchards) yet his mother's insistence on his regular attendance at Sunday School brought him many much-loved books, several of which I still have. When he was twelve years old he wept copiously over *A Peep Behind the Scenes* by Mrs O. F. Walton, given him in 1894 for Regular Attendance and Good Conduct.

In the street Father spoke the local dialect which was condemned in his home, but it certainly enlarged his vocabulary. He was exposed to the foul language and thoughts of some of his play fellows, and also saw more of the seamy side of life than his mother suspected. The educational value of the various dramas that were played out in his home by visiting relatives made school seem boring, but he must have displayed some ability there for the Headmaster, 'Pa' Elliott, used him increasingly for collecting registers, delivering messages etc. After ten years at school Father could read, write legibly and spell accurately, manipulate numbers of enormous size, and knew all the tables in existence (including the apothecaries' table of grains, penny weights and ounces). Literature, science, history and geography were closed fields.

In his fourteenth year his mother withdrew him from school, and sent him to look after his older brother John's business that was currently in decline. He was there eighteen months. During one winter, out of boredom, he attended the local technical school on one evening a week for a course on building construction. Then, quite suddenly, on the recommendation of his ex-headmaster, he was summoned to an interview with the chief printing firm in Macclesfield. He was appointed to their new lithographic department, and signed the articles of indenture to an apprenticeship for six years at a wage of six shillings per week, rising annually by one shilling a week. For three years there he did monotonous work cleaning and 'feeding' the machines with paper. A work day lasted nine hours, but in his second year he started going to evening school. There he got his first indication that education could be enjoyable, and at the end of the year, to his surprise, won first prize in the class. He chose for it Green's *Short History of the English People*: it still sits in his study. He then increased his variety and speed of reading, and became absorbed in the classics, starting with Lamb and de Quincey and W.H. Hudson – a mixed diet, but he recalled it as glorious.

At the age of eighteen years he consulted his older brother Will, for by then he was appreciating the latter's exceptional qualities. His mother managed to get him out of his apprenticeship, and he and Will worked out a programme of a year's work to prepare him for a Queen's Scholarship which would give him admission to a university or a teacher's training college. There were fifteen subjects to be taken, and of the algebra, geometry, science and a foreign language he was completely ignorant. His old headmaster invited him to join the daily 8 a.m. class he held for pupil teachers in his school, when he heard them repeat the tasks given them the evening before. The first morning's task for Father, set the afternoon before, was to learn the definitions, postulates and axioms of Euclid. It took him two mornings, but after that he absorbed the First Book of Euclid at the rate of one Proposition each evening, presenting it orally next morning with the help of the blackboard. All this was an illustration of Butler's dictum that before a boy is made to learn a piece of knowledge he must feel that he cannot get on without it, and certainly Father felt this. Modern education has lengthened school life in an effort to teach more, but surely even more important is the pupil's attitude.

Father then persuaded the authorities to allow him to become a pupil teacher for one year, rather than the regulation four years. His salary was to be £15 per year. He also joined a correspondence college, answering weekly test papers. Then in December came the Queen's Scholarship Examination, held over four days in dim gas-lighted rooms in a slum school in Manchester. Father passed the examination First Class, and was bracketed twentieth in the list for the whole country. He could not join the University until the next October, 1903, so he had nine months to fill in. He decided to go to France to improve his knowledge of French.

Will's great friend, Uncle Sydney Moore, had been out in France in 1899, working in a school in Nontron, so Father was able to follow him, going out to the Dordogne as an English Assistant at the *École Primaire Superieure et Professionelle.* The headmaster provided board and tuition for 40 francs a month, and Father lodged in a room over a shop opposite the school for a further 10 francs a month. (This totalled 10/- per week.) Many families in the town were willing to pay 2/6d per hour for private English lessons, and so Father could pay his way.

In January 1903 Father sailed from London to Bordeaux, accompanied by a large tin trunk full of extra clothing and heavy books. He suffered from seasickness but recovered by the time they sailed with the pilot boat up the Gironde river under a full moon. Nearly fifty years later the memory of the beauty of it was still crystal clear in his mind.

The school had five teachers and about one hundred boys in it, taking a three year course leading to employment as junior civil servants etc. Food was spartan – the main dish at most meals was haricot beans eaten with a hunk of dry bread. In 1971 I visited the school, and found it had not altered much from Father's day. It was May, and still bitterly cold at nights. In a classroom the desks were arranged in tiers, their rows rising up the sides of the room, with the master sitting at the bottom by the side of a tortoise stove. The floors were stone, the equipment simple. The only thing that warmed me was the friendliness of the greeting I received, and the gift of an armful of wild lilies of the valley that the headmaster's wife gave me to bring back to England.

Father had much freedom. He could attend or avoid lessons as he pleased. He explored the district taking long walks. He found caves with prehistoric drawings in them, into which he crawled on his stomach along narrow passages, unrolling a ball of string behind him so that he could find his way back to civilisation. He hired a bicycle, and explored the neighbourhood, getting to know the shepherds, the charcoal burners, the peasant women tilling the ground, the labourers in the vineyards, the washerwomen on the riverbank, and the ropemaker, the wheelwright, and the blacksmith, all still using simple tools and age-long methods. Life had changed little through the centuries. There were reported to be wolves still roaming the woods, and Father took the headmaster's dog with him on walks – a brave step, as he shared the Smith dislike of dogs. He never saw a wolf.

This idyllic life ended when Father learnt that the Cheshire County Council had announced the offer of eight university scholarships for competition, each worth £50 a year, for three years. He was determined to enter, though he knew the competition would be fierce. In the ferocious heat of Southern France he worked with a will, returning home to England three days before the examination in July 1903, after having been only six months in France. The number of scholarships had been raised to nine, and Father's name came out ninth in the list of successful candidates. He was nearly twenty-one years old, and owed his success to his old headmaster, an evening school teacher who had inspired him in history and, in addition, his own self-education. He had devised a system of analysing and arranging the essentials of a subject until he got them clear, and then memorising the result. Had he been born thirty years later, his future would have been decided at the age of eleven years by the educational system. As it was he had arrived where he wanted to go, with a good deal of experience in life.

At Manchester he first of all read science, the only course open to one who knew so little Latin, and in two years took his B.Sc., and then returned to his real love, the arts, taking his intermediate examination for a B.A. degree at the end of his third year, and in his fourth year getting an honours degree in Literature and History. Thus in four years he had obtained two degrees and a First Class Certificate as a qualified teacher. He played no games and had little leisure, but he had been involved in the Debating Society, attended the theatre, and in summer watched the giants playing on the County cricket ground.

Father then taught for three years, first at West Bromwich Secondary School (1907 – 8) where a colleague called Carroll used to ask him home to tea. He was allowed to nurse his host's little daughter, called Madeline, whom he saw many years later playing opposite Robert Donat in *'The Thirty Nine Steps'*. After West Bromwich he was a Demonstrator for two years at the Fielden School in Manchester. In 1910 he went to Cambridge for two years as an 'Advanced Student'. There he had £30 from an exhibition he had won, and he was earning a little by journalism. His mother, now in easier circumstances, made him a gift and his sisters, Ann and Edith, by now teachers, let him have interest free loans. So in 1910 Father entered Emmanuel College Cambridge – always called 'The Borstal' by Uncle Jock (The Revd. J.O. Kennedy, Father's great college friend.) Father decided to spend his two years in Cambridge doing research in experimental psychology, and thought for some years a new weapon had been forged for educational advance. He only had two compulsory lectures a week in his own subject: other lectures were open to all students, and he revelled in the short courses given by famous scholars in English Literature and philosophy and social theory. Serious and stimulating discussion went on among the students by day, and often far into the night, and Father participated fully. Lazing in punts and skating on the Fens in winter did not harm his work, and he obtained his M.A. degree.

He then taught French and English for one year (1912 – 1913) at Sir John Dean's Grammar School, Northwich: he called this 'a year's imprisonment and undiluted misery', for the school was run on tyrannical and narrow lines. Rescue came when at the end of 1913 he was appointed Lecturer in Education and Master of Method at University College, Aberystwyth, and had a very happy twelve years there. It was a progressive college and colleagues, friends and students were receptive to new ideas. There was time to discuss these, as well as to explore the stimulating and unspoilt countryside. He wrote his life of Sir James Kay-Shuttleworth, the first Minister of Education, which Sir Michael Sadler spoke of as 'the classical biography of one of the founders of public education in England.' It was published in 1923, after nearly three years of work. It was commissioned by Sir James' son, the then Lord Shuttleworth, who befriended my father and entered into the work wholeheartedly: he wrote my Father 133 letters about it, plus memoranda and lists, and crates of papers accompanied my Father to and from Barbon Manor and Gawthorpe as the research continued. It was the calibre of this book that helped my Father to get his first Professorship in 1925, at Armstrong College, Newcastle upon Tyne.

Eight hard working years in Newcastle followed, for this was the era of mass unemployment on Tyneside. He was unsparing of himself, and became first chairman of the newly established Tyneside Council of Social Service, and first chairman of the Tyneside Nursery School Association, as well as Assistant Commissioner of Rovers. In spite of his leadership in voluntary social work, besides being heavily involved in the developing work at Armstrong College, Father published in 1931 his *History of English Elementary Education, 1760 – 1902*, which also became a standard classic. He also wrote eighty-eight front page articles and a number of leading articles for the *Times Educational Supplement* between 1923 and 1938. These were unsigned, but it emphasises how influential he was in the English educational field. It was also a useful financial addition to the family budget, so in 1930 we got our first car – VK 1818, a fifteen horsepower Armstrong Siddeley saloon.

In 1933 Father became Professor of Education at Leeds University. He was delighted, for one of his old Manchester teachers, whom he greatly admired, was Sir Michael Sadler, who had been Vice Chancellor at Leeds and was one of his referees for the job. His new Education Department was much bigger, but he still wrote – e.g. the section on the Nation's schools in *A Century of Municipal Progress, 1835 –*

OUTSPOKEN LEEDS PROFESSOR.

REFORMS HE WANTS IN EDUCATION.

"**E**DUCATION fails in our time because it provides no permanent life interests. By giving too much and on too easy terms before 14, and too little after 14, it allows its work to be undone," said Professor Frank Smith, the new head of the Department of Education at Leeds University, in his inaugural lecture last night.

"We have entered into a machine age in very truth, and the leisure which the 19th century destroyed so carelessly is now returning to us almost too abundantly," he said. "The chief victims of the present position are the boys and girls of 16 and upwards. We are just beginning a period when the output of the schools at 14 will increase owing to the increased birthrate in post-war years, and an industrial world does not want them."

"There are areas where emergency measures are wanted for conditions that may yet disappear, but the increase of leisure is universal and permanent. It is a fact that education cannot ignore, and our national system is sadly wanting in the equipment it gives to the vast majority of our adolescents whereby they may withstand the snares of a life that may make little call on their self-respect, their interest, or their efforts.

"The problem is largely one of readjustment from the sheltered and directed life of the school to the unsheltered and unstimulated life without, and the chief cause of maladjustment is the abruptness and completeness of the change.

"The school must not develop an all-absorbing life within its walls and remain cut off from the opportunities outside."

USES OF THE CINEMA.

Professor Smith suggested that the cinema had helped to transform popular amusements, while the traditional school attitude was to instal the apparatus in school for teaching and to ignore or lament the different kind of teaching that went on so vigorously in every picture house. Experiment on the use of cinema halls as a direct educational provision was needed.

The pre-school child also needed help. There was an unsolved problem in the provision for very young children in the poorer quarters of large towns. It was estimated that a million such children lived under conditions that made help almost impossible. The remedy was available in the nursery schools that existed in lamentably small numbers.

"The supreme need of the present time seems to be a national Council of Education, more permanent than a Government Department, more representative of the different phases of life than Whitehall and endowed with more initiative and responsibility than the present Consultative Committee of the Board of Education.

THOSE WHO COULD HELP.

"There are three groups in this country who have a unique contribution to make to educational policy. The administrators at Whitehall have access to information from the whole country and long experience in organising their national system, but are cut off from the human side of the educational problems.

"The local education authorities have thirty years of administrative experience and intense local knowledge; and, third, there are the teachers, whose knowledge of the human lives that are being influenced is so detailed and so rich.

"A combination of the three groups would bring phases of experience together which would give to policy a wiser, steadier, and more permanent advice."

1935 (*The Economist* said his chapter was 'outstandingly successful'). He wrote forewords for several books, and then in 1939 the section on Elementary Education for the *Encyclopaedia Britannica*. He was in great demand as the speaker at school prizegivings (I have cuttings from thirty of them). In 1935 he became a Fellow of the Institute of Handicraft (that meant summer schools for us all at St Annes-on-Sea and Chester) and Professor Cyril Burt (whom he did not like) made him a fellow of the British Psychological Society in 1942. He was President of the Association of University Teachers in 1934, his Presidential address being a plea for Freedom of Speech as a primary requirement of intellectual life. He chaired an International University Conference in Oxford in 1934, when I met Maria Montessori, who grudgingly gave me her autograph, and Ishbel MacDonald, the Prime Minister's daughter. He addressed numerous conferences on such matters as 'The Needs of Youth', and to my pride he was President of the Salt Schools, Shipley, from 1935 – 1936, following such illustrious names as Professor Gilbert Murray, Winston Churchill and Ramsay MacDonald. The list is endless: suffice it to say that when he retired in 1947 he was also Pro-Vice-Chancellor of Leeds University, and on fifty-six committees, being chairman of twelve of them. He was also Governor of six schools.

I must add two other items. Firstly he was chairman of the appointments committee for Leeds General Infirmary. When I collected him from meetings, driving his big car (by then KY 9414, a 19.8 horsepower 1935 Armstrong Siddeley) porters sprang to attention on every hand, giving me a very exotic view of hospital life. When I later became involved in the National Health Service, I found a very different world!

Secondly he was Chairman of Council of Abbotsholme School, a public school standing in one hundred and thirty-three acres by the lovely River Dove in Derbyshire. It was founded in 1889 by Dr Cecil Reddie, and designed for one hundred and twenty boys from eight to eighteen years of age. It was 'to retain the character-building emphasis of the great English schools, while clearing away some of the conventions and artificialities which threatened to stifle them. The curriculum was modernised and liberalised: the compulsory subjects were chosen to meet the basic physical, intellectual, artistic and moral needs of the individual.' Physical needs were met not only by games but by outdoor work on the farm, the garden, and workshops. Academic standards were not sacrificed to the examination fetish, but small classes were designed to develop a boy's individuality, with a strong foundation of the curriculum being based on English language and literature. Dr Reddie was a pioneer of his time and his forceful personality left a mark on education that aroused great interest all over Europe and America.

My Father joined the Abbotsholme Council in 1935, and was chairman from 1946 – 1951. He loved it. Colin Sharpe, its outstanding headmaster, also saw the aim of education as 'the development and enrichment of personality.' Modern Abbotsholme is now co-educational, with two hundred and fifty boarders and day pupils, aged eleven to eighteen years.

The school council had long cherished a plan to develop a group of schools on the Abbotsholme plan, and in 1947 purchased an estate three miles away, called Doveleys. My Father got the Duke of Devonshire to perform the opening ceremony on 1st October 1949. To the boys' intense excitement the Duke arrived at the school by helicopter – a very dashing and innovative event in those days. Unfortunately the number of parents who could afford high fees dwindled in the face of the economic realities of the time, and Doveleys School closed in 1953. Maintaining two schools in the same neighbourhood, both with falling numbers, was too great a risk so the two schools were amalgamated.

Those who worked with Father recognised that his treatment of the History of Education introduced the majority of his students to the basic values of human society and human achievement. They found him good to work with, with warmth of heart and a strong sense of humour beneath the surface. His lectures were characterised by clear, logical exposition, while his kindliness, sincerity and humanity endeared him to both colleagues and students. He saw education as a great social welfare movement, but he saw it too as safeguarding and developing a great intellectual and traditional national heritage, and felt it was as important to secure diversity to suit individuals as to secure equality of opportunity. As a chairman (and this was especially appreciated in the University) he kept complete control of the proceedings, and never obtruded his own views unduly. He was absolutely just and impartial in giving judgement.

Chapter Nine

Aberystwyth

As I have said, my Father was appointed as Lecturer in Education at the University College of Wales, Aberystwyth, in 1913. He at once married my Mother, and after much sadness over my sister Gwyneth's death, I was born on 7 November, 1916, into what became the happiest of homes. My Father, obviously being as economical as possible, announced my birth in a terse telegram to Granny at Langley: 'Eve and Winifred both splendid, Frank'.

My childhood was idyllic, in spite of the illnesses that dogged my Mother and myself. I ate no solid food until I was five years old, as my muscles had not developed properly and swallowing was a problem, so my early years were haunted by ill-health, and I was trailed round a succession of doctors, specialists and masseurs, all of whom tried to cure my general sickliness, my frequent attacks of tonsillitis and constipation and what, many years later, turned out to have been appendicitis attacks, but were then called 'liver upsets'.

My Mother gave up her music in order to nurse me, but she also was dogged by illness, and the onset of the crippling rheumatism that increased with age. Mysterious gynaecological disorders involved her in visits to yet another group of Manchester specialists, and two attacks of rheumatic fever in Aberystwyth meant that our summer holidays, always spent with Granny in Macclesfield, also encompassed stays at the spas of Buxton and Trefriw. Buxton was fun: it had lots of desiccated and speechless old ladies sitting under rugs in wicker

71

basket chairs; these had a small wheel in front with a handle attached, so that the old lady could control the steering. Horsepower was provided by tottery old men, who pushed the chair from the rear, up and down the Broad Walk. The total effect was very impressive, and I watched in awe.

We stayed in rooms just off the Broad Walk, where we bought the food and the householder cooked it for us. The landlady had a daughter called Dorothy, slightly older than myself, who played games with me, and introduced me to the joys of Marmite spread on bread and butter. I thought it was the most wonderful innovation. Dorothy also had a silver wrist watch, but it was a few years before I managed to coax one costing 8/6d out of my parents' slender purse.

The first day in Buxton was a revelation, for the market place had a man in it selling a great bunch of many-coloured balloons. I found difficulty in choosing the colour I wanted, and disappointment when I got it in my hand, but it was a lesson in that I realised one colour by itself was a poor thing compared to the many hues bobbing about on their strings. Suddenly I heard a tremendous noise, and a fire engine in full regalia dashed across the market place. I had never seen one before so Buxton, at once, to my mind, became a place of wonderful happenings.

I do not remember much of the Trefriw holiday in the Conway valley, except that it rained a great deal, and there was thick mud on the roads. It seemed that the chalybeate (or iron) waters ran outside as well as inside the pump room, and everything seemed damp.

My 1908 *Guide Book to Trefriw* likens it to the great continental spas of Marienbad, Aix là Chapelle, etc, and gives an impressive list of the afflictions it could cure. These included Mental afflictions (e.g. melancholia, low spirits etc.), Torpidity of Digestive Processes, Chronic Rheumatism, Sciatica, Debility, Constitutional or Hereditary Diseases, Diseases of Mucus Membranes, Chronic Skin Diseases, Diseases of the Nervous System and the Eye, Worms, etc. It was also beneficial for 'female complaints', and a whole list of other illnesses. Mother found it all too drastic and used to emerge pale and limp from the baths, so we never went there again. Nor do I think did she gain much improvement in health.

It must have been about the same year that my Father went to do some summer job in Paris, in so great a heatwave that people were said to be dying like flies. One night he attended the opera and saw *Madam Butterfly*. The part of the heroine was sung by the fattest woman he had ever seen in his life, and it gave him such a dislike of opera that he never again would go to a performance.

There were many days of fun and beauty in my childhood. In my memory the Aberystwyth of my youth was a land of sunshine, for one forgets the days of illness and trauma. So many things I still remember clearly – for instance I can describe all the flowers in our garden there. The short path up to the front door was fringed with a Karl Druske rose, with a great bed of sweet violets growing under it that we gave away in bunches to friends. Along the front wall to the pavement were three pink China roses that always seemed to be in bloom, but our crowning glory was at the end corner, against our party wall with Mrs Richards. This was a vast lavender bush that filled about one-sixth of the garden: visitors going past used to stop and exclaim at the scent. By the front door, in soil so dry that one wondered how they survived, were a clump of bright red carnations, and a mauve clematis that climbed up the wall over the doorway. The two steps leading up to the front door were the home of ants who used to come out through the cracks in busy platoons. Exasperated by their numbers Mother sometimes attacked them with disinfectant and kettles of boiling water, to my Father's horror, but the army of ants never decreased. I was fascinated by the way they removed bits of stick and leaves, and used to crouch down watching them. If I upset one of their manoeuvres the ranks quickly reformed and resumed their task.

Indeed Aber. seemed to be heavily inhabited by livestock of various kinds. The back garden had more ants than soil, and snails in their lovely shells crawled up and down the ferns in the dark corner by the dining room window. Once when some flagstones were lifted in the back yard a great mass of wriggling woodlice appeared. Voracious slugs devoured the fruit on our strawberry bed, undeterred by the straw that Daddy carefully placed round it, in a vain attempt to save the fruit for us. Walking into town in the hot sun in the summer was an adventure, for hornets sunned themselves along the top of the convent wall in Llanbadarn Road, and you had to dodge any movement they made towards you. If you sat on a seat on the promenade (so hot it burnt through your combinations, knickers, petticoat and dress) you always caught a flea – or perhaps I did because I was a plump victim that looked appetising to them.

To a small girl it was all very exciting, if dangerous, and yet our street, Iorworth Avenue, looked a most placid and quiet place. (When the house was bought Mother wrote home to say 'It is nearly in the country but if there is a big storm at sea you can hear the roar of the waves crashing on the shore, and sweeping great mountains of sand on the promenade.') The road had not then been made, and was covered with grass and mud: opposite our house was a field where a donkey lived, and I was allowed to take it an occasional treat of carrots. There were only two pairs of semi-detached houses built in Iorworth Avenue then, and we lived at the third house called Underwood. My particular friend was kind Mrs Richards, who lived at the second house, and who wore shapeless hand-knitted silk jumpers that stretched dangerously across her large bosom. She had a trellis in her back garden up which climbed a rambler rose, and a wonderful collection of white and mauve sweet-smelling pinks in her front garden. She and her husband were Cockneys, with Cockney accents, and they took in lodgers. A Cambridge friend of my Father's who came to teach in the town lodged there for a time, and brought with him, in the early 1920s, a wireless set. The night before he arrived Mrs Richards came to see my Father in great secrecy after dark – did he think it was safe for the set to be in the house? He reassured her, but she was very nervous of this new-fangled invention.

My friend Barbara Perkins, whose father was head of the Electricity Works and who bred bulldogs, had a wireless set and I had been taken to hear the Children's Hour on it. All that came through was an orchestra playing grown-up music and I was bored stiff, for I was not musical, and had expected something more exhilarating. I loved to hear Mother play the piano at home, for I felt so proud of her, and everyone told me how superb she was. She took me to hear a rehearsal of the new Welsh Symphony Orchestra, playing in the College Hall, Queen's Road, Aberystwyth, for Sir Walford Davies was Professor of Music at the College, and he organised many music festivals. Mummy explained I was not to be frightened of the drums. I found them alarming, but this was counterbalanced by the importance of having the conductor, Sir Edward Elgar, sending his score down to Mother to follow during the rehearsal of the Enigma Variations.

Sir Walford was a great character. He and the Principal of the College gave a staff children's party each year, and this was a Big Event in my life. I was a fat and heavy child, but I can remember sitting on their knees while they worked hard trying to get me to talk to them. I was too shy – I used to become quite silent when out of the family circle, to Mother's chagrin. Sir Walford and Lady Davies lived outside Aberystwyth, and he drove a car. (This was a mark of importance in those not-so-distant days.) Always rushing, he would drive into Aber to catch the London train, arriving just as it was getting up steam to leave. As he tore down the platform and leapt into the moving train he used to shout to the stationmaster, 'Go and park the car somewhere.' This, to me, made him an impressive person. I knew how important he was for Sammy Langford (SL of the *Manchester Guardian*) came down all the way from Manchester to the Musical Festival each year, so as to report it in the *Guardian*, the paper for which my Father had much veneration. Sammy and Mrs Langford and their daughter always came to have tea with us when they were on these trips, and musical erudition was the order of the day. This was an age when children were still very much seen and not heard, so I kept as silent as a mouse as they munched their way through Mother's lovely home cooking.

Our other neighbours in Iorworth Avenue included some who were highly dramatic. At house number 4 there was a succession of owners, including the Hutchens, who moved to Bournemouth. My chief memory of them was of their elderly daughter uttering the classic phrase to Mother: 'Pa must have his cow-cow' (cocoa). This became a family phrase, my Father uttering it in a shrill, falsetto voice, always reducing me to giggles. The arrival there of the Revd. and Mrs Richard Morris gave a new importance to the street. He was a Godly man, who kept a harmonium in his back bedroom upstairs, on which he occasionally played hymn tunes, the noise of which filled my bedroom with discordant sound. Mrs Morris was his second wife, whose chief claim to fame was that when he proposed marriage to her he took her to the local cemetery and said: 'Here my parents lie. Here my wife lies. Here I shall lie. Would you like to lie here too?' She accepted him.

He spoke very slowly, enunciating each word carefully in a sing-song Welsh accent. The introduction of the Cinema to Aberystwyth intrigued him, and he resolved to go and see this new amusement. For the first time in his life he encountered tip-up seats, and in the darkness perched himself on his seat which was still folded up. Indignant cries from behind urged him to 'sit down'. With great dignity he twisted round, and in his deep resonant slow voice replied, 'But I am sitting down'.

At the bottom of our street lived old Miss Rowlands whom everyone agreed that even by Aberystwyth standards was a little odd. She had a succession of very Welsh-speaking and scared looking maids, none of whom stayed long with her. Perhaps this was because she got them to scrub out the coalhouse every week, carefully moving the coal from one side to the other in order to facilitate the operation. Her drawing-room had the first Indian carpet I had ever seen, with an ivory-coloured background (everyone else in Aber had sensibly coloured backgrounds). Miss Rowlands spent her afternoons, when the sun shone into the room, in nipping round the carpet, moving large sheets of brown paper over the floral patterns, to prevent them fading. Years later, when I read *Cranford*, I felt myself back in her room. Mother and I went to have tea with her sometimes, and once when I had a newly-decorated bedroom the current little maid trotted up the street with a grey pottery bowl for me, filled with white and mauve pinks. The message was that she had got the bowl in Florence – this baffled me, for although I had an aunt called Florence I had never heard of Italy. I still have the bowl among my treasures.

Down Llanbadarn Road, beyond the Convent, there was a small sweet shop manned by Mrs Payne, who had a young invalid son who seemed to be about six feet long, and who lay completely flat in a wicker-work invalid carriage that she pushed him about in. I was terrified lest I get as long and as pale and thin as he was, for I saw my elders shaking their heads over his fate, as he continued to elongate. My business relationship was with his mother. She sold me sweeties, and my father used to give me one shilling to buy him a packet of twenty Wills Gold Flake cigarettes. Mrs Payne and I then had very important negotiations to carry out over the counter. I collected Wills cigarette cards, so together we opened every packet in her shop in order to find the cards I had not already got. Nowadays Environmental Health Officers would condemn the whole proceeding, and close the shop forthwith, but in the early 1920s life was much less sophisticated.

It is strange how I remember my contemporaries by their gardens and their flowers. The Ifor Evans boys, Eric, Melvyn and Denys, lived in Carreg Wen with pink rhododendron bushes on the lawn – the only other place I saw these were in my Grandmother's garden at Langley. The boys had a great big rocking horse, and a large collection of scooters and tricycles on which we used to rush round the house, always avoiding Uncle Ifor's gleaming car which we were not allowed to touch.

Up Caradoc Road, at Willow Lawn, lived the Douglas Lauries. Mary was a particular friend, as were both our parents, for Uncle Douglas was in the throes of forming the Association of University Teachers. He was its first secretary, and Father was the publicity officer, so communication between the two homes was non-stop. He was also Professor of Zoology, and when wasps and hornets nested over his front door or in the porch he would not dream of destroying them – visitors had to duck smartly into the house via the French windows in the drawing room to avoid the stings.

Willow Lawn was a small detached dream of a house, approached up a drive that was curtained with syringa, so tall that it interlaced over your head, while shimmering sunshine dappled the lawn, and the air was full of perfume. Even by the 1930s it still had no electricity, and when staying there we went to bed by candlelight, wildlife streaming and fluttering in through the open bedroom windows. The soft Welsh air was so full of the scent of roses that one longed for it never to change, so perfect did it seem.

Mary Laurie was younger than me, and also an only child. I greatly admired her decisiveness and ability to solve problems. Her steps were dogged by a succession of foreign governesses, most of whom she seemed to resent. How well I remember the Garden Party her mother was giving when Mary, exasperated by some orders of the current fraulein, locked the latter in the summer house, and threw away the key! The wooden summer house vibrated with passionate teutonic shouts and bangings from within as the guests arrived, and as poor Aunt Laurie tried various keys in the lock. I would never have dared to do such a thing myself, but it engendered in me an admiration and an affection for Mary that has never faltered.

Later the Lauries moved to a house full of mystery, called Crugiau. It stood down a long drive, with a whispering clump of trees at the gate. When you reached the house there was a wonderful triangular view of the sea, and you could hear the faint sound of waves. The mystery lay in the house's history, for it was thought it could have been a smuggler's haunt. Auntie Laurie, digging in the garden one day, hit what she felt could be the roof of an underground tunnel running down to the shore. The house itself was exciting, for she had opened a slender cupboard door by an upstairs fireplace, finding inside not only shelves, but also remains of winding stone steps going downwards in a spiral. The drawing room also was quite a different measurement inside from out – about a quarter of the room was missing. Unfortunately the Lauries only rented the house, so could not demolish walls, but I was in my teens, and well-stuffed with romantic stories about secret passages, and longed to explore. Unlike the school stories I read I never seemed to get a chance to discover hidden treasure, for a few years later our next door neighbours in Leeds had an old house with a rumoured secret passage running from it to Kirkstall Abbey. How I longed to probe their cellar with torch and chisel, but I was never allowed to! Their younger son assured me he had looked carefully, but this did not satisfy me: how many of us always feel that if *we* did the job, it would make the luck change!

The greatest treat was to go on walks along the promenade to gaze out to sea, for I had been told America was out there, but it was too far away from Aberystwyth to see. I was always sure that if I peered hard enough that one day I would be the first person to see it – but alas this never happened. Another walk was round the castle ruins where white bladder campion and pink sea thrift grew on the walls. Or we might go up to the National Library of Wales, passing Webb's Nurseries at the foot of Caergog, where we could buy a whole armful of border carnations for 6d if we were feeling rich, and Mr Webb sometimes gave me a few red baby tomatoes that had dropped off the plants by accident. Oh, the lovely smell of those tomatoes!

At the side of the library was a field, for in those days the terrain had not been ruined by the new functional University buildings that have been built, where once my Father showed me a lark's nest. Admission to the field was by a small wicker gate which had a large notice on it saying 'Private'. My father sometimes marched us through the gate for the field was a carpet of wild flowers, and he seemed to have no fear of Mr Bracegirdle, who was the custodian of the grounds, and who terrified me. (I was a very law-abiding child, a trait that has bedevilled me all my life.) I suffered agonies in case Daddy went to prison, while at the same time I was longing to go and roll in the flowers. Mrs Bracegirdle was a subdued and quiet woman who made the loose covers for our drawing room Chesterfield and easy chair: I never remember her speaking, but Mr Bracegirdle did, especially if he met us in his field.

'Penny for the first celandine,' was Mother's cry as we set off in

Spring to walk up Penglais. It was a dusty road, with a dusty hedgerow in which on one famous occasion the first celandine had turned up unexpectedly on New Year's Day. In those days telegraph wires were on tall poles by the side of the road, and they used to hum loudly as you passed underneath, each pregnant with undecipherable messages. There were few cars, for carriages and governess carts were still all the go. Our drive home from the station after our summer holiday was always in a carriage: the driver, a woman, wore a species of jodhpur, which I thought highly immoral – as, I suspect, did most of the town. Before we left Aber in 1925 she had however changed over to driving a taxi cab, but I do not remember how she dressed for that.

I do remember clearly the excitement of being taken rides in motor cars. A two seater was driven by Dr. D.J. Saer (who with my father and John Hughes made a study of bilingualism: they wrote a book on it in 1928 for which the college awarded my Father a Ph.D.). On one momentous occasion Dr. Saer took us all to see the vicar of Hafod whose daughter had been one of Father's students. Mother sat with Dr. Saer in the cab of the car while Father and I sat in the dickie. Half-way there there was a cloudburst: Daddy put his umbrella up and we cowered under it, while the water rose over our feet. Occasionally I saw Mother's alarmed face peering anxiously at us out of the small talc back window that was in the cab. We were none the worse for it though.

On another occasion Dr. Ernest Jones, our beloved general practitioner, who was later Medical Officer of Health for Aberystwyth, saw Daddy and me one Sunday morning walking up Penglais – my first outing after an illness. He was motoring to Borth to see a patient. 'Hop in,' he shouted. So off we set to Borth. He was a long time in the patient's house he visited, and I spotted in a little closed shop a small steam engine that actually worked, and which I would have liked. It helped to divert me from my anxiety about Mother not knowing where we were, and sure enough when we got home she was frantic with worry, and our Sunday dinner was burnt. Luckily she had not known with whom we had been or her alarm would have been even

80

greater, for she had not got a very high opinion of EJ's driving. He was an old Cambridge friend of my Father's, and though she greatly admired his professional skill, she learnt that when he bought his first car the previous owner showed him how the gears worked, but forgot to tell him how to put the car in reverse. EJ drove off up the road, eventually wanting to turn and go back: never short of ingenuity he stopped, opened a gate into a field, drove in and around, emerging to face homewards. Somehow this story had not given Mother much confidence in his driving skill.

We all loved EJ. He spent many evenings with my parents during his bachelor days, and was a great tease. Once when his friend Martin Lloyd Jones (who at that time was a Harley Street specialist later going into the Church and becoming a famous preacher) was staying with him they came round after dark and approached our house quietly. They were armed with three or four snails that they stuck on the drawing room window panes, and then stood back to await results. My parents, sitting in innocent and blissful silence indoors, were panic-stricken by the sudden eerie screeching noises that came into the room as the luckless snails tried to climb up the glass. There was no clue as to where the noises came from, but eventually the culprits, convulsed with laughter, rang the front door bell. My other memories of EJ were happier: he did most of his courting at our house, for Rhiannon Morris-Jones was often there, and although he was older than she was he was swept off his feet by her charm and her monocle. Her mother, Lady Morris-Jones, rushed to Aberystwyth to ask Mother if she thought the match would be happy. In the event it certainly turned out to be.

The college abounded in eccentrics and I wish I could recall the name of the lecturer for whom Father was so sorry, and who was totally unable to keep order during his lectures. One day the students decided that they would not let him give his lecture that day, and put into operation an elaborately worked out plan. As soon as he mounted the rostrum a student got up, and in a carefully worded speech, proposed that, as it was stuffy in the room, a window should be

81

opened. Before the lecturer could get a word in, another student rose, and seconded the motion. This was put to the vote and carried. At once another student rose, proposed that Mr X should open the window, and gave reasons as to Mr X's suitability for the job. This was seconded and carried. Mr X then opened the window and the lecturer thought he saw an opportunity to speak himself. Not so. Someone got up and complained that there was now a draught. This was seconded and agreed, and someone else's name was put forward to be the closer of the window. In this way the whole of the lecture's hour was filled, while the hapless lecturer sat almost in tears.

Another young lecturer, a psychologist called George Green, was regarded as very *avant-garde*. He painted the walls of his sitting-room black, and wore canary yellow waistcoats – I was even embarrassed to be seen speaking to him in the street, so many were the curious and shocked glances thrown at him. Remember this was an age when correct and subdued clothes were worn. Even I once nearly died of shame when I wore long black woollen stockings and my button boots were brown. The strictness of Sabbath observance, and of etiquette in dress was rigid: funerals were attended only by men, all clad in black, even their handkerchiefs having black borders.

A particular friend of my Mother's was a Frenchwoman, Madame André Barbier, (wife of the French Professor), who was a delightful and exhilarating companion, although some found her formidable and tactless. Unfortunately I did not know her, for she did not speak to Mother for thirty years, because Mother did not christen me Lucie, after herself. She also eloped with Professor Alfred Zimmern in 1921, the then Professor of International Politics. This caused tremendous scandal. To me she was a legend, but many years later I saw her when Sir Alfred Zimmern came to lecture in Leeds, accompanied by Lady Zimmern, ex-Barbier. She seriously embarrassed the chairman of the meeting, Professor John Harvey, by rising to her feet and announcing she would prepare the audience's minds for her husband's talk. She spoke brilliantly for twenty-five minutes, and I found her much more stimulating than the lecture given by her husband. Later she came to our house, having apparently forgotten that I was not called Lucie, and propelled herself across our drawing room carpet at speed, straight into Mother's arms, shouting 'Darleeng!' I watched entranced, for she did not look like the *femme fatàle* that I knew she was, as she was elderly, short and plump, but I came to the conclusion that her mental brilliance was what charmed men to her side, and that alas I could never be destined for such an exciting lifestyle myself.

In October 1923 the then Prince of Wales visited Aberystwyth. By great good luck I had my first encounter with Royalty, for Mother and I were on our almost daily walk up Penglais and heard by chance the trot of hooves, and there was just time for me to exchange waves with him in his carriage before he disappeared down the hill in a cloud of dust. I wondered if he would be taken to see that sad grey Union Workhouse at the bottom of the hill, where no window was ever opened and where no one ever sat in the garden. The place was a source of never-ending wonderment to me, for the high surrounding wall was topped with broken glass. I was never sure if it was to stop desperate inmates from trying to escape, at dead of night, or if it was to prevent small boys from climbing in, but I think the Prince was only being shown the beauties of the neighbourhood.

Mummy then told me however that His Royal Highness was on his way to visit the college, and that afternoon there was to be a tea party in his honour, at Alexandra Hall, the women students' hall of residence. Clad in our best bibs and tuckers, we duly turned up. There was a complex tea-time plan: the Prince was to have tea with the Principal of the Hall and a number of the favoured few. After HRH had helped himself to a piece of very splendid cake, it was to pass round the room. In an adjoining room the staff wives were to have tea, the remainder of the cake being pushed through to them surreptitiously when the Prince was not looking. They were thus not able to see the Prince, but still seemed flattered at being allowed to share the same cake. Staff children, as the lowest in the peck order, were relegated to a basement room to have their tea, and were deprived of both a sight of the cake and the Prince. 'Now you are not to be afraid,' Mother said firmly, 'I'll fetch you after tea.' We had never been parted before, so soon after I was settled in my seat downstairs I burst into tears. Nobody could control my heartbroken sobbing, so eventually I was taken up to Mother, who I think must have been very ashamed of her ewe-lamb's behaviour. I did get a crumb of the famous cake however, off Mother's plate, though I assure you that had not been the reason for my distress.

School for such a delicate child as I was obviously presented problems. My first school was at home where the Ifor Evans boys came round to do brushwork with me under Mother's guidance. This was a failure: we were all very tiny, and the boys wept loud and long for their Mother after she managed to sneak out without them seeing. (Eric died in the last war, in Tunisia in 1943: he was nominated before he was killed for a Military Cross for conspicuous bravery.) Soon Aunt Verna Gelly appeared on the scene – at first she held her school at the Ifor Evans house, and then it moved to the YWCA at Haul-Fan, Terrace Road. It was on my Father's way to college every morning, and he used to walk there, taking me. I always blamed my habit of walking in long strides on this walk, as I struggled to keep pace with him all those years ago.

Auntie Verna was trying to make a living after her husband, Joey (later Mathematics master at Dolgelley Grammar School), came home from the war and was, I think, temporarily jobless. They became our life-long friends. It was a happy little school of about nine pupils, and I loved it. I still have the egg cosy in the shape of a cockerel that I made there.

The next stage was going to the junior school at the convent, 'St Padarn' in Llanbadarn Road. The nuns were mainly French and tried to teach me very fine embroidery and how to sing Frères Jacques in French. Soeur Françoise was always convinced I knew French because both my parents were such good linguists, but I have always been a duffer at languages. Mother's Wesleyan family were horrified at me going to a Roman Catholic school, but it was the best infants' establishment in Aber at the time. It also had a private bluebell wood whose scent filled the neighbourhood in the Spring. We were told that there was a snake in it, but I always thought that was to keep us out. Sometimes the Mother Superior took us in for a treat. I had a navy uniform and felt very adult. I had just moved up into the senior school at the age of eight years when we left Aberystwyth. I could then read and write, draw and paint, but I had quickly sensed that the senior school was miles above my then mental capacity after so many lessons missed through illness.

A favourite treat was to go by train to Borth, a small hamlet seven miles north of Aberystwyth, with its row of cottages almost nestling on the beach. Some years we took rooms in a cottage there for a week, but although Mother never lost her love of the place, it did not treat us very well. The first year we were there a woman tried to drown herself in the middle of the night. It was pitch black, and from the sea came her screams and the shouts of men wading out to pull her in. The next time we stayed there I developed a very high fever in the night and wanted a drink of water. Our landlady locked the door at night leading through to her quarters, and all Father's shouts and bangings on the door went unheard.

Recounting these stories to the local schoolmaster's wife, we were at once invited to go over again for lunch – and to see how normal Borth was. So Mother and I set off from Aberystwyth. It was a lovely day with blue sky and a sparkling sea. As we were early we walked along the beach, much puzzled by a very large wreck ahead of us. Closer inspection revealed a dead cow, washed up by the sea, and swollen to gigantic proportions!

Borth had one famous shop, which its enterprising owner advertised as 'The Harrods of Borth'. He introduced into Wales large inflatable rubber animals you could ride on in the sea, and he sold spades with proper metal blades, so that the young making sand castles could do it much more professionally. After the total eclipse of the sun in 1926, he issued a postcard of 'The Eclipse as seen from Borth.' It was just a blank.

Borth achieved fame in 1876 when Uppingham Public School,

under its headmaster Dr Thring, was evacuated there, during a serious and deadly epidemic of fever at the school, due to drains. On 27th March a special train of eighteen trucks decanted three hundred beds and bedding on Borth's tiny platform, followed on 4th April by 290 boys plus masters, in three different trains. Borth then consisted of three-quarters of a mile of straggling buildings, ranging from mud cabin to stately hotel. The latter was hired, and sixty to eighty boys overflowed from it into the village in billets, mostly kept by poor widows. The problems of feeding, washing and heating were overcome by the kindness and welcome of the local populace, but many problems remained to be mastered. For example, how do boys work and play in winter evenings with an inadequate supply of candles and smoking lamps? The rumour in my family was that the boys, in gratitude for the hospitality they received from their hosts (many of whom had no English and still dressed in traditional costume) built a path with disused sleepers across the bog that lay behind Borth and Ynyslas. It had superb views of the Dovey Estuary and was full of wild life treasures. In the Spring it had big patches of wild yellow iris in flower. It usually shimmered with heat in the summer, and on at least three occasions we found Ynyslas wooden railway platform smouldering, just recovering from yet another fire, so fiercely did the sun beat down on its wooden planks.

I have left until the end of this chapter an account of my dear, dear, Mary Jones. Mother and Father had moved into Underwood just before my birth, and Mary then arrived as their maid. She was with us until I was seven years old, and she was part of my life. When she left us to marry Jenk, who worked as a farm labourer for 15/- a week and a pint of skimmed milk on Sundays, she slipped out of the house when we were at supper, leaving the three of us round the dining-room table. Two of us were choked with sobs, knowing that the kitchen would be empty when we went to it. Together Mary and I had read *The Rainbow* every week, following the adventures of Tiger Tim breathlessly, and she was the comfort and solace of all the house. Earlier she had been engaged to another man, and when he came home from the Army on leave, they had planned to go off for a day together. When the day came she would not leave Mother's side, as I was having one of my acute illnesses. He went on the trip alone, and brought back two handkerchiefs, one for her and one for 'the little girl'. He was killed soon after he returned to the Army.

When we moved from Leeds to live again in Newcastle in 1947 she came for three weeks to help us to get straight. We might never have been apart, for we had always kept in close touch. She had never been out of Wales before, nor had she been in a lift, and said, as she stepped out of her first one, 'I wondered what you were taking me in that little box for!' As Mother said, she would have followed us to the gates of Hell. It was to see her that I went to Wales after my Mother died in 1967, and I still miss her kindness and loving letters most dreadfully. She helped so much in those Aberystwyth days when there was practically no money. University lecturers were paid a pittance then: most of Father's salary went on paying doctors' bills.

Among my Aberystwyth memories I remember the magnificence and beauty of Cardigan Bay, and the fishcart that came to our house with the fish so fresh on it that an occasional one still gave a convulsive leap on the cart. I remember too the farmers who came into Aber from the hills, some only Welsh speaking, so that Mother had to buy eggs and chickens by sign language at the front door. I remember the music in the voices, and the kindliness that surrounded me there. Wales is still to me a land flowing with milk and honey, where Mummy's friend, Lillian Bowker, on her first visit bought a tin pail to take it back to Manchester full of the magnificent blackberries that so charmed her. Mary would go off to Cwm Woods in the afternoon to bring back a basin full of wild strawberries. Many of these things have gone, but I have only to shut my eyes to feel my cheeks fanned by the soft Welsh air coming through the open carriage window of the Cambrian Line train, as it puffed along going down to Aber, and bringing me nearer and nearer to the paradise it was to me. I drove back there after the War and stopped at the top of Penglais. Aber looked like Lilliput stretched out below, but to me it is still a giant as I pull back the curtains from my memories. I have never forgotten I was brought up by the sea, even when it became angry, and from the safety of my bed in Iorworth Avenue I could hear the distant roar of the waves, lashing the promenade in a storm. It enriched my experience of growing up. I often think I ought to live there again, sensing anew the ultimate power of the elements, and feeling revitalised in the clean salt air, while the rain-washed clouds, scudding across the Atlantic, hurl themselves on the West coast.

Chapter Ten

Newcastle upon Tyne, 1925 – 1933

In 1925, after a determined and fruitless opposition to the idea of leaving my beloved Aberystwyth, I was won over by the prospect of packing my nightdress, slippers and hairbrush in a microscopic cardboard attaché case I then owned. Also we were to stay overnight on the way North with Uncle Sydney and Auntie Florence, at Silcoates School. It was going to take two days for the furniture van to travel from Aberystwyth to Newcastle, and Silcoates was a useful half-way staging post for us. Lil, our current maid, shared my dislike of leaving Wales, but after she had bought herself a heavy topcoat, with a large fur collar, which she showed me in the secrecy of the broom cupboard, she obviously had also changed her mind, and travelled with us.

We had a great welcome from Uncle and Auntie, but my chief memories are of Lil, when she assisted at waiting at table at supper, hissing at Mother 'Don't eat any!'. It turned out that she had seen Auntie's handmaiden in the kitchen stirring the junket with filthy fingers, and then licking them before the next stir. The other memory was Auntie Florence's assertion that in the cellars of the house you could hear the miners talking as they went about their work in the coal seam that lay below.

My Father, on being appointed Professor of Education at Armstrong College, Newcastle (later the University of Newcastle) had asked Godfrey Thompson, his predecessor, whether his house was up for sale. 'No', said Godfrey, 'my solicitor bought it, but his is up for sale in the same road.' Father at once inspected it, and bought it on the spot, so when he got back to Aber he had both an important new position and a house. I was told that there was a swing in the garden, and the Town Moor was over the bottom hedge. Bliss! I knew the Cat and Fiddle Moors near Buxton very well, and I envisaged games and camp fires in the heather, so I was heartbroken when we arrived to find only grass and not a gorse bush in sight! The swing was fun, only I was having one of my frequent bilious attacks when I first rushed to it, and felt sicker and sicker as it moved back and forth. But I saw from it, as I flew upwards, my first tramcar, advertising the *Daily Mail* on its side.

The removal had been relatively smooth. A small crowd, weeping copiously, had mustered at the station at Aberystwyth on 3rd November, Mother and I contributing our share to the dampness. Mrs Richards had taken into her house our troublesome cat Smut, and the future seemed trouble-free, once we had steamed out of the station.

Two days after we arrived in Newcastle on 5th November, it started to snow, and continued to do so, on and off, until March. I had never seen snow before, and initially liked it, though Mother and I had a series of chills and took to our beds regularly. That spring Mother decided she must take me to see the North Sea so, accompanied by Lil, we went to Roker. It was enveloped in a cold, wet, dense sea fret, and we got lost on the sands, unable to see where the land lay. Lil then went back to Wales. In the summer, on a warmer day, Daddy hired a car and driver, and we went out to see the Roman Wall which everyone talked about. We had lunch at The George at Chollerford and then walked in warm sunshine and a biting East wind by the River North Tyne – it was a lovely outing.

I was sent to a small local school, started by Dr Gertrude Hickling, wife of a famous Professor of Mining, George Hickling. The school was run for the benefit of their younger daughter Margaret, and about nine of us went up the road each day for lessons in their comfortable schoolroom. Ever afterwards I associated it with Longfellow's poem, 'Hiawatha', which was read aloud there. The dining room I always remembered by its mid-morning milk, which was followed by a piece of apple 'to clean your teeth'. Dr Hickling, who was doing pioneer paediatric work with the legendary Sir James Spence, was particular about health matters. It was a most happy time.

From this school I progressed to 'Goodies' (Miss A. Robyn Goodrich) who with two other teachers ran a private preparatory school in St Monica's Church Hall in Wingrove Road. We had visiting teachers for singing, dancing and piano. Had I been in better health I would have learnt more. As it was I had frequent tonsillitis, liver attacks, measles, scarlet fever, chicken-pox for the second time, numerous colds and chills, and double mastoid – Dr Frank Wilson saying that if he operated I would be deaf for life in both ears. This illness had developed a week after I had been inoculated for smallpox, and my ear drums swelled out of my ears. The pain was a loud continuing pounding in my head, which I kept saying was like Tegsnose Quarry, near Granny's. Luckily it abated. So my schooling was very intermittent – but I had learnt to read. My Father had given me Charlotte Young's *Book of Golden Deeds* when I was too small to lift it, but now my Mother stepped in, and produced her old copy of *Little Women*. I soon abandoned her reading it aloud to me, for I was so eager to know what happened, and I suddenly found I could read anything! My boast was that I could get through four and a half books per day, when I was confined to bed. I drew the line at some authors: I only enjoyed Walter Scott when Daddy read *Ivanhoe* to me, for he missed out all the heavier historical bits, but for myself I had discovered schoolgirls' stories and, in particular, Elsie J. Oxenham. Her delightful *Abbey Girl* series made me long to folk dance. About then Armstrong College staff started a folk and morris dance group, and as I was aged fourteen, I was allowed to join with Mother. We went weekly to our class, and even got to a folk dance festival at Blagdon Hall where Douglas Kennedy, head of the English Folk Dance Society, gave a demonstration. I got his autograph, and that of our host, Viscount Ridley, who glared at me ferociously when asked.

My parents were also in the Armstrong College Staff Dramatic

Society, my Mother distinguishing herself as the landlady in Hades, in Aristophanes' *The Frogs*. Father, dressed as a knight in armour, (dishcloths sewn together and painted with aluminium paint) appeared in *Orme of Edendale*, a Northern play being given its premier and, as far as one knows, never again being produced. To my eternal shame I took part in a Tableau, dressed up as the fat boy in *Pickwick Papers*, my morale not improved by the convulsive giggles of other staff offspring in the audience who had managed to evade inclusion in the performance.

My last school in Newcastle was the Central Newcastle High School, (Girls' Public Day School Trust) from 1930 – 1933. My Father chose it because he preferred the headmistress, Miss Hiley, to the then headmistress of the Church High School, Miss Gurney (known to her scholars as Old Sal). In those days the two schools were deadly rivals, the Church High considering itself the superior in every social way, Miss Gurney even castigating one pupil before the whole school for carrying a basket in town when she was wearing school uniform. The CNHS got excellent examination results, with a large proportion of the girls going on to distinguished university careers. Miss Hiley, who was a brilliant Oxford graduate, should have stayed there as a don, rather than going into teaching. The sixth form however found her an invigorating teacher, but she only took the middle school for scripture, and I learnt very little from her. She would give a lesson on some very obscure piece of theological theory and the next week spend the whole of the lesson telling us how her grandmother had nearly married Sir Walter Scott. She could be very sarcastic at times, and I even trembled when her gaze fell on me. Mother, Dr Hickling and Mrs Leslie Hunter, wife of the Archdeacon of Northumberland, all decided that there was too much homework being given out, and the other two decided that Mother, as wife of the Professor of Education, should beard Miss Hiley in her den. Mother was very thrown by Miss Hiley's reception of her, for she pointed a stiff forefinger at a chair, and said to Mother 'You may sit Thar'. Mother lost the battle. Miss Hiley was most curious too in some ways. When I left the school, at the age of sixteen years, she wrote to my Father saying 'We shall be sorry to lose our nice old Winifred'. This comment made me splutter with rage, and Daddy roar with laughter. She could hurt people too: she wrote some very unpleasant letters, one of which I saw recently. Some thirty years later I saw her at a school reunion, and she said, 'Oh, I often wondered how you turned out.' I'm sure she saw me as a failure. I only achieved fame once in the school when, at the age of fourteen, Dr Grey Turner removed an enormous bursting appendix from my stomach, saying if he had been half an hour later I would have died. He took it straight down to the Medical School and gave the students a lecture on it. Close interrogation by the curious young at school as to what it felt like to be dying fell flat though. All I could recall was the waves of pain, intermingled with the sight of our general practitioner, Dr Worthington, rushing in to see me several times in the evening. He was clad in white tie and tails, for he and his wife were trying to attend a ball.

This last illness led to most of my teeth going rotten and being extracted, so the remaining front two upper fangs made my parents call me 'The Walrus'. I had to have false teeth. I continued to have my numerous chills, colds and tonsillitis attacks, but my parents did not want me to have my tonsils out, as Cousin Bun had his done before he died of pneumonia in 1925. Of the three years at the CNHS I was absent for two of them in total.

Mother, after careful thought, took me to the theatre for the first time, choosing *Lilac Time* as being suitable. At the end I was discovered in floods of tears, and bawled, 'She should have married Schubert!' At the other end of the scale, also about the same time, a trip to see Charlie Chaplin in *The Gold Rush* was arranged, at the Grey Street cinema. I roared with laughter so loudly that a strange man, sitting on the far side of Mother, urged her to take me out, in case I harmed myself. So between illnesses there was a lot of fun, but I was still not strong enough to enjoy more than short walks. One day we took a bus to Ponteland, had tea in a café, and set off to walk home. After a few steps I stopped and said 'I refuse to go one step further!' Nothing would budge me, and Verna and Joey Gelly, who were staying with us, kept reminding me of this phrase until they died. We caught the bus home. On the whole I managed to cope with never being able to do much. Goodie had called me 'philosophical' one day: I rushed home to ask what it meant.

We got our first car, an Armstrong Siddeley 14 horse-power, in 1930. Daddy had lessons from a Mr Yendal, who unwisely took him on to the newly opened coast road. Daddy wanted to see how fast the car would go, and pressed the accelerator down to the floorboards. Mr Yendal emerged from the lesson pale and shaking. The car opened up even more the magic of Northumberland, with its castles and Roman remains. Until then we had relied on friends to take us out. The kind Mr and Mrs Phillipson showed us the county, their daughter being a lifelong friend, and the Hicklings also helped, though Mother was always nervous of Professor Hickling's driving. She had been in his car across Newcastle Town Moor with two lines of traffic going either way, Professor Hickling buzzing cheerfully along as a fifth lane in the middle. It shook her faith in him, especially as at a later date he crashed his car in the Pennines when he had my Father as a passenger. They both took it quite calmly, arriving home after 3 a.m., apparently unharmed.

Wonderful picnics took place, and we grew to love the area. One superb day, in snowy weather, after hearing a report that there was skating at Ryton-on-Tyne, we went there in our new car. I was muffled in rugs on the back seat, cuddling a hot water bottle, as I was just out from an illness. There I saw Father transformed. He had learnt to skate on the frozen fens near Cambridge, and his stocky figure suddenly became a darting skimming bird, as he cut figure eights and did wonderful arabesques among the other skaters.

In addition to our usual summer trips to Langley, we now started having Easter holidays away. One year it was Bournemouth, with walks up and down the chines, watching grey squirrels play in the trees; another year to Torquay and Newquay in endless Northerly gales, Mother so glad of the fur coat she took, even though my Father had said it would not be necessary. One year it was Gatehouse of Fleet, in Scotland, with the lanes carpeted with primroses, and then again Harrogate where Mother ate suet pudding daily because she said it warmed her tummy.

Happy though we all were, life on Tyneside was not pleasant for many. I had gradually become aware of the collapse of the economy, and the social distress that lay all around me. Going in a train through Durham in 1926, and seeing pit ponies enjoying life in the fields hurt me, when Father told me they had never seen the sun before, and as soon as the miners' strike was over they would go back underground for the rest of their lives.

Mining and shipping slumped, and mass unemployment and poverty surrounded us. The Principal of Armstrong College, Sir Theodore Morrison, handed over to my Father his place on the Bureau for Social Research on Tyneside, which grew into the Tyneside Council of Social Service. Father was its first chairman, and Henry Mess was director. He and his Norwegian wife, Sophie, became friends. One Sunday afternoon, going to have tea with them, we surprised their household in some confusion. Apparently Dr Mess, in a gambit to keep his children quiet while we were there, had given them an advance Christmas present of a box of guaranteed harmless chemicals. Just before we got there they had blown a large hole through the kitchen table. Dr Mess, who was an inspired sociologist, moved on to become Lecturer in Sociology at Bedford College, London. During the War, when his children were evacuated to Masham in Yorkshire, he used to stay with us in Leeds when he was *en route* to see them. One visit coincided with a stick of bombs landing unexpectedly near Masham, to his alarmed surprise.

I well remember the poverty in and around Newcastle. Barefoot urchins ran in and out of dark, dank alleyways off Gateshead High Street, and small carts, driven by even smaller ponies, tugged impossibly large loads up the steep streets of Tyneside. Their owners, usually huge men, sat on top of the load, often using the whip unmercifully. Overcrowding in the bad housing of the area brought illness and despair in its wake. In 1920, 1922 and 1924 Gateshead had the highest death rate from tuberculosis in any county borough of England and Wales: in 1923 and 1925 South Shields claimed this doubtful honour. Twelve per cent of the Gateshead population lived in one room in 1921. (It was 3.6 per cent in England and Wales). The Tyne was famous throughout the world for the quality of its products, but this did not save the populace from the effects of the economic slump of the 1920s and 1930s. Jarrow, built almost entirely below the 100 contour line, relied for work on one employer, Palmers. They had the largest ship-building business in the world, and when trade crashed and their yard closed, the town was left without any future hope of work. Yet Dr Mess found the Tyneside people full of strong local pride. On the other hand J.B. Priestley, visiting the area in winter, 1933, found the Geordies 'stocky toothless fellows in caps and mufflers, cursing in their uncouth accent'. However, he had influenza and a temperature, and was dosing himself with belladonna at the time, so perhaps he can be forgiven.

Unemployed coalminers and shipyard workers (many of them skilled craftsmen who had served long and faithful apprenticeships) trudged into Newcastle each morning to try to find work. I saw them clustering round every street corner, sitting on their hunkers, leaning hopelessly against walls and shop windows. At night they trudged home again, penniless. It was an agonising time of hardship, for the Unemployment Assistance Board did not come into being until 1934, to assist those whose unemployment insurance had been exhausted. It was then too late for many proud and independent souls.

The Tyneside Council of Social Service opened community centres in all the Tyneside towns, often built by the men themselves. There the unemployed and their families could come, and either just sit in warmth and peace, or they could learn new skills. The men at Hebburn built a boat, and went out on the Tyne to fish. Drama, opera, and classes in every conceivable subject helped to broaden horizons, so did camping holidays.

The Tyneside Nursery School Association, of which Father was

96

also the first chairman, came into being. In a moment of generosity I gave my adored Teddy bear, worn rather bare in patches, to Bensham Grove nursery school. I still regret it, and dream sometimes of his reproachful gaze. The secretary of the Nursery School Association was a painstaking and devoted woman called Mrs Wardley-Smith, who made long evening calls to our house to discuss committee plans with my Father. She spoke deliberately and incredibly slowly, her most cherished sentence being 'Things... are... moving ... very ... swiftly.'

Among the visitors who came to Tyneside was Margaret MacMillan herself: she went out to Kirkley Church to preach one Sunday night in 1930, and we went to hear her. What the villagers made of nursery schools and her views on the education of children I have never discovered, but Lord Kirkley was full of ideas for improving the rural mind. Shortly after he got Father out to preach there. After the service he invited us all in for 'A cold collation'... ('What's that?' I muttered in Daddy's ear). Apologising for the butler's absence (two housemaids tried to make up the deficiency) I gazed in awe at a sideboard creaking under the weight of game pie, ham, tongue, beef, lamb, etc. etc. After the meal my parents had liqueurs, my mother plumping for crème-de-menthe which she had heard of, but not yet tasted. She was speechless for a time after the first gulp, and Lord Kirkley took me round the drawing room to show me various pictures, each lit by an electric light above, something I had not seen before. This was my first evening meal in a really elegant manner, and I was excited by it all.

Visitors to the Tyneside Council of Social Services abounded, and many came to stay with us, among the most notable being Eleanor Rathbone, who came first as a Parliamentary candidate, Daddy being one of her sponsors. Then after being elected she came as a Member of Parliament for the Combined Universities, and was a close friend of Mother's. She later ran a one-woman battle throughout the country to get Family Allowances legalised, which were to be paid to the mother of the child. (Remember that pre-War women had no rights

97

and no money of their own.) When the Family Allowance Act was finally passed, she was given a celebratory dinner by Members of Parliament of all parties. Later I knew her when she was deeply involved with the Duchess of Atholl in work for refugees from the Spanish Civil War. She used to send wonderful telegrams; one sent in 1935 read: 'Agree eleventh inadvisable have London meetings twelfth considering my Leeds functions tenth and sixteenth think might abandon election meeting will phone you or Happold tonight. Rathbone.'

To our regret the two seats for the combined English Universities were later done away with, and she and T. Edmund Harvey (another Leeds friend) who held the other seat, were no longer in Parliament. Their strength had lain in contributing highly intelligent and impartial comment to Parliamentary discussion.

Eleanor's last poignant Christmas present to Mother was a copy of *Another World Than This*, by Vita Sackville-West.

Our other 'principal' visitor was Brigadier General Sir Wyndham Deedes, CMG, DSO (1883 – 1956) who had ridden with Allenby into Jerusalem at its surrender on 11th December 1917. After leaving the Army he became vice-chairman of the National Council of Social Service at a time when the National Council had tremendous influence in the country, especially in areas of deprivation. Mother was a bit apprehensive about putting up a Brigadier General for the night, and prepared a most excellent roast fowl and trimmings for dinner, only to discover he would only eat a sausage. His favourite meal, as we came to know so well, was tea and a biscuit. Compton MacKenzie, in *Gallipoli Memories* has some fascinating accounts of Sir Wyndham out there, where he was running the counter-espionage service, besides being in charge of the interpreters, for he spoke Turkish perfectly. He took MacKenzie on what he called a 'quiet county walk', when for two hours they walked through a large barrage of shrapnel and shells on a beach. He was perfectly serious – Sir Wyndham was able to ignore discomfort and become so absorbed in his thoughts and discussion that he was oblivious of his surroundings.

I found him to be very observant if he so chose, but he could only get through all the work he undertook by complete absorption in each question he tackled.

The younger son of a distinguished family, after Eton and service in the Rifle Brigade he had gone out to the Near East for five years, as an inspector in the Turkish Gendarmerie. He learnt to speak and write Turkish probably better than any Englishman of the century. All through the 1939 – 1945 War he broadcast weekly to Turkey on the BBC World programme. He had a distinguished military career, and later an equally successful administrative role, culminating as Acting High Commissioner for Palestine. But in 1923 he voluntarily relinquished all the power and distinction, having felt for some time that it was his duty to help his fellow men. The Balfour Declaration and a study of the prophetic books of the Bible made him want to press the case of the Zionist cause, as he tried to revive Anglo-Israel friendship. He also devoted himself to work in the East End of London, living in Bethnal Green, and to countless national organisations that were established for the good of man. His working day usually lasted nineteen hours, even after a major illness in 1954, when he continued his practice of writing letters in bed from 2 – 4 a.m. and from 6 a.m. onwards.

When 1939 came he was pressed 'by the very highest' to take up an important war appointment in Turkey, but he preferred to remain in London, which he saw as the future battleground of any war. From 1939 – 1945 he was Chief Warden for Civil Defence in Bethnal Green, and Chief Information Officer for London. He made light of the bombing; a 1940 postcard says: 'Two friends with the initials HE were left on the pavement opposite my doorstep, and he shook the dust off his feet into my 2nd storey rooms! And so on thro'out the Boro, and of course the Riverside copped it worst. But we are all tails and thumbs up. I shall come to you by first train .... when I can.' I have a mental picture of him inspecting his shelters and Wardens' Posts during a bombing, impervious to the crashes round him – a repetition of the Gallipoli days.

He was a saintly man. He and I wrote dozens of letters to each

99

other, meeting as often as we could, and revelling in one another's company. When Father died in 1951, Wyndham wrote: 'My beloved Friends. You fill me with grief. No home surely was ever more beautiful than that of you three – so devoted to each other. I can well believe that you both feel utterly shattered. My heart goes out to you.'

Wyndham had a capacity for writing in Cockney (I replied in Yorkshire), and a sense of fun that not everyone was permitted to see. Once, when motoring past the Hotel Majestic in Harrogate, its signboard read 'Dancing Every Night'. 'That's where we should be staying, Win,' he said, knowing that I knew that it would be the last place in the world he would enter.

It is perhaps forgotten now that Citizen's Advice Bureaux were his brainchild. He founded them in 1938/9, to help the man in the street how best to deal with family and personal problems during wartime. They are now part of our culture, and a fitting memorial to a man of such forceful ideals and integrity, whom I still miss acutely.

Another visitor who came in and out of our lives, but more like a comet, was J.J. Findlay. He had been Professor of Education at Manchester in whose experimental Fielden School Father had taught. JJ was now old, but his enthusiasm never dimmed: in 1930 he was busy getting gramophone records made by foreigners to teach children how to speak a foreign language in an authentic accent. (Mother said his own French pronunciation was awful). He was also forgetful; once he descended on us on a Sunday to catch the Norwegian boat from the Tyne early on the Monday morning. He had forgotten to get the visa that was required! A consul had to be roused from his Sabbath slumbers and turmoil ensued, but JJ was finally put on the boat.

I have not said much about Armstrong College. It was small then; my Father's Education Department had five lecturers. Of the men Vernon Brown was senior, and often Father had a policy of appointing young ex-public schoolmasters to his staff. An early lecturer was J.F. Duff. He later, as Sir James Duff, was Vice-Chancellor of Durham University, and Lord Lieutenant of Durham County. He used to tell how alarmed he was on his first day in the Department, when he saw a door at the head of the stairs marked 'Pure Mistress'. This referred to Miss Ellen Melville, Lecturer in Education and Mistress of Method, and a perfect dear. She had prominent front teeth and a petticoat that had an unfortunate habit of hanging in an irregular line beneath her dress. She lived with her sister, Selina, in a small house they had built on a new estate outside Newcastle called Darras Hall. She drove a small two-seater car. Selina, who was a tiny crippled woman, painted quite well, and they used to go on expeditions driving at a stately speed into the countryside. Both had an acute fear of the car running backwards on a hill, and as Nellie's driving seemed to involve such a slow gear change that they frequently did stick on hills, they carried a brick with them to put under the back wheel. Unfortunately this meant Selina getting out, putting the brick in position, and then when the car moved off, carrying it up to the top of the hill, so as to regain her seat in the car. So they attached a stout cord to the brick, Selina hauling it in as they chugged up. Later they built a small shack at Gunnerton, some twenty-five miles from Newcastle, so that they could take their holidays in the countryside, and paint in peace. The first night they slept there they were terrified, as a farmer's cows crowded round, rubbing themselves luxuriously on the iron sides of the shack.

Another delightful lecturer was Stella Bailes, who built a most artistic small house almost next door to the Melvilles. She collected china robins, and although she seemed prim, at student parties she used to recite Hillaire Belloc's *Cautionary Tales* in a way that had her audience shouting for more.

I was becoming more and more aware of my Father's importance. He was a member of the City Education Committee: his speeches and lectures were praised to the skies. His leadership of the Tyneside Council of Social Service at a time of intense social distress was outstanding. When he appeared on a newsreel, dwarfing the Prince of Wales, whom he was showing round a centre for the unemployed, my excitement grew. He participated too – he led a group of youths who met each Sunday afternoon in the stables at the Bishop's house at Benwell Towers. He became an Assistant Commissioner of Rovers but he stipulated that he did not wear uniform. This was all right until he went to the World Scout Jamboree at Arrowe Park in 1929. He was driven there by our friend, the Revd. R.H.L. Slater, head of Toc H in Newcastle, and whose tired little car finally collapsed in the ditch as they reached Liverpool. It is most likely still there, for it was never heard of again. At 10 p.m. everyone not in uniform was turned out of Arrowe Park, and as Daddy was staying there, this presented difficulties. One man found a big pair of shorts, and another produced a pullover that had run in the wash, and which served to cover all the gaps, so the day was saved. The Northumbrian Rover contingent seemed to be made up largely of miners, who then cooked a pot pie, for their appetites were legendary. Father refused it, having been satisfied with his supper, but as he did not wish to appear stand-offish, he asked if he could have milk and a biscuit. They brought him a seven pound box of biscuits and a quart jug of milk.

One of the joys of my parents' lives was of being members of a Reading Circle that met monthly. After a reading by one member of some book (carefully expurgated by the reader), they discussed it. The fascination lay in the membership. There were several elderly male Richardsons, linked to the Leather family, all unmarried, and all great characters. Mother, sent upstairs to take her coat off by one of them, was solemnly assured that the room was ready for her, as her host had sent out for a packet of pins and a box of hairpins with which to furnish it. There was an old lady with an ear trumpet that let out shattering wails at times: other hearing aids that attended were less strident, but seemed to have a life of their own. There was my Geography mistress, who lisped ...

In short, it was a relic of Victorianism at its best. My parents used to come home and rush up to my bedroom where I was lying waiting for them, my cat Whiskers warming my feet, so that they could re-enact for me the highlights of the evening. They were never cruel – they just enjoyed the oddities to the full.

In 1929 an unprecedented upheaval broke out in the University of Durham's Medical School in Newcastle. The Professor of Comparative

102

Pathology, Professor H.J. Hutchens; DSO, MA, MRCS, LRCP, & DPH, appointed for life by the University of Durham in 1908, was dismissed by the University Council from his post as Lecturer in Comparative Pathology. He had an unchallenged reputation as a teacher and scientist. Their decision was based on the recommendation of the Committee of Enquiry who did not give him an opportunity to hear the evidence against him. They formulated no charges against him, found no fault with his work, and gave no reason for his dismissal! Professor Hutchens and his supporters submitted that the Committee was not impartially constituted and that a summary dismissal of this kind would make the position of persons employed in the Universities intolerable.

After 1926 the administration of the College had been altered, and a committee had discussed the merging of the Bacteriology Department with the Royal Victoria Infirmary, to form a conjoint Institute of Pathology and Bacteriology. Almost immediately two of Professor Hutchens' assistants were dismissed, and in 1928, on the ruling of the President of the College, it was agreed that the Department be divided into two parts. While Professor Hutchens was away on vacation, one of his assistants was made Director of the Public Health Laboratory, and given full control of the building, nearly all the staff, and made directly responsible to the College Council. Professor Hutchens was left with one part-time assistant. After he objected, a Committee of Enquiry was set up in 1929. The membership of this Committee was one of the most important matters of dispute, and again Professor Hutchens had no access to its evidence nor could he bring witnesses to it. It was publicly stated that Sir Robert Bolam, Registrar of the College of Medicine, secured three bought governorships there, so as to influence the voting. Locks were changed on the doors of Professor Hutchens' department and his papers, books and equipment moved by night, without his knowledge.

The bitterness spread, with the Association of University Teachers fully supporting poor Professor Hutchens who, heartbroken, bewildered and practically penniless, refused to give up the fight, after twenty years of distinguished service. My Father and two colleagues, Professor Hickling and Professor Briscoe, held interminable evening meetings to discuss strategy. Father brought in Sir Norman Birkett, an old Cambridge friend, as legal adviser. At Father's Presidential address to the AUT in London, December 1933, he said: 'University teachers everywhere are being called upon to defend the University idea and ideal from attacks that are full of danger. Freedom to teach, freedom to learn, freedom to investigate – these are the primary requirements of intellectual life, and the history of our universities clearly shows that their denial brings stagnation and death.'

In developing this theme, Father went on to say, 'Yet a large City Council (Newcastle) is at this moment in serious conflict with an English university, and is demanding an impartial inquiry into its statutes and administration, following upon the dismissal of a university teacher for no ascertainable cause, and upon the scandalous method adopted by a group within one of the constituent colleges of buying seats on the Court of Governors for their friends and relatives, in order to defeat the intentions of publicly elected representatives.'

It was a sorry story, leading to the 1935 Royal Commission in Newcastle which merged the College of Medicine and Armstrong College as King's College, a division of the University of Durham. It was full of guile and manipulation, which would have been much relished by C.P. Snow or Trollope. Professor Hutchens, who had an invalid wife and a son in a sanatorium in the South, was given a small job on the staff of the city's Medical Officer of Health. He was never re-instated.

Our house was always full of people, or so it seemed. I drew the line at child psychiatrists (then coming to the fore) for I said they all had liquid brown eyes that peered hard at me. In 1931 a month after my operation for a bursting appendix, Daddy got on the train at King's Cross one night to come home, and was smitten with an agonising pain. He made the journey, drinking whisky and soda (which he never did normally) and collapsed out of a taxi at our front door at 11 p.m., Mother getting the doctor at once. Again Grey Turner operated (offering to do Mother cheaper for the quarter dozen) for Daddy's appendix really had burst. He had peritonitis, and for a time his life hung in the balance. But he recovered, and scarcely able to totter, came home. We hired a chauffeur and drove to Cliftonville, near Margate, Daddy and I sitting on the back seat on air cushions. The apple orchards of Kent were in full blossom – it lay like snow on the branches, and the hotel where we stayed overnight in Windsor the lilac was in full bloom. Three weeks on the chalk cliffs at Cliftonville transformed us all back to health.

Chapter Eleven

Leeds, 1933 – 1939

Father was particularly pleased by his next appointment as Professor of Education at Leeds University, which he saw as a much larger and more challenging job. Also his salary, on appointment, was £1,000 per annum. The current Vice-Chancellor was Sir James Baillie, a philosopher and an affable Aberdonian, who lived in great style at Bardon Tower. His wife, a niece of Lord James, was very dignified and a stickler for etiquette. She expressed great horror that Mother allowed gentlemen to smoke in the drawing room.

Leeds brought a new dimension into our lives, for it was so cosmopolitan after the then extremely narrow-minded rivalries of the small townships of Tyneside. I was sixteen when we moved, and adored Leeds, for to grow up in such a big city of commercial and artistic success was a revelation to anyone of my age. My cup was full the first night there, for I went on a tramcar in Headingley (the district of Leeds where we lived) and a man and a woman in full evening dress – he wearing a cloak and collapsible gibus – joined the other passengers on the lower deck because their car had broken down. Never had I seen anyone as exotic on a Newcastle tram! To be honest, never again did I see it on a Leeds tram. To me it was like a gate opening on another world, full of wonderful experiences waiting to be explored. By now I had accepted as the norm the snobbishness of society, and was developing into a being who was ready to die of shame if I or my parents were not dressed correctly. In the thirties a long evening dress (accompanied of course by long white kid evening gloves) was *de rigueur* for dances, as was a full-length dress and picture hat for garden parties. Choices of suitable hats and dresses for day-time wear were equally important. I also learnt that invitations to gentlemen for dinner containing the phrase 'short jacket' meant the wearing of a dinner jacket, and not a white tie.

I was increasingly confused at not knowing where I really fitted into society's peck order, so I was tossed between revelling in the new life I was expected to lead, and shame when anything or anyone broke the rigid laws of etiquette. Ladies still called on one another and left visiting cards for themselves and their husbands and Mother was always ready with afternoon tea set out at teatime: the bread and butter had to be wafer thin, with superb little cakes from Betty's to grace the occasion.

Father's appointment brought him fresh honours. At first we lived in a small flat for a year, while the University made up its mind whether or not to appoint him as Warden of the Men's Hall of Residence, Devonshire Hall in Cumberland Road, Headingley. His predecessor as Professor of Education had also been the Warden, and the University did not want to appear to be creating a precedent. Originally the Hall had been two large grey stone houses, standing in extensive grounds in Cumberland Road. One house, Regent Court, had been run as an hotel until the University acquired it; the other house was to be our home. The architect, John Proctor (brother of Ernest Proctor, the artist) had designed the Hall on the staircase plan, reminiscent of Oxbridge, so the two houses were cleverly joined together in a series of buildings joined together by cloisters. There were rooms for one hundred and forty-five men students to be in residence. The staff consisted of twenty-five maids, plus nine men servants (five porters under a head porter, Mr Young, in the porter's lodge, which was manned day and night, two gardeners and a handyman). There was a matron, an assistant matron, and two lady cooks. If we had unexpected guests for a meal, or a special menu was wanted for a distinguished house guest (like the Archbishop of York) we simply picked up a phone and ordered it. All our food was cooked in the Hall kitchen, and the two house parlour maids allocated to our personal needs carried it into our house on big trays to the hot plate in the dining room – they always served our meals and waited at table. We had no kitchen in our house, but we had, besides the dining-room, a large study and a drawing-room over thirty feet in length. The staircase took four abreast, and was topped by an enormous glass dome, christened by Mother the 'cockloft'. We had seven bedrooms, three bathrooms, and four loos in our house.

The first morning there I came downstairs to breakfast and saw a huge bunch of multi-coloured asters and roses on the hall seat, the dew still on them. It transpired that the head gardener always brought a fresh bouquet in every morning so that the Warden's wife could do the flowers in our house. Mother soon altered that – her flair for flower arranging was not going to be dismantled daily! Also she disliked throwing out nearly fresh flowers. We then discovered that there were six doors leading through from our house into the Hall, and after Mother had caught some strange young maids coming out of her bedroom she remembered Mrs Strong, the previous Warden's wife, saying she was leaving the Hall with an empty jewel case. Our closure of the majority of the doors was much resented.

So – we had arrived! Mother always said we lived like minor Royalty, and it gave her the opportunity to be a superb hostess, always kind and thoughtful to our guests, she was also a brilliant conversationalist. Father dined in Hall with the students four nights a week, but the rest of the time ate with us. Outside our house there was a large lawn with cloisters on two sides of it, and an immense old bird cherry tree standing in the middle. That tree was a joy in blossom time, and a lovely sunshade when later in the year, during the summer vacation, we had strawberry teas under it. Its only drawback was that quantities of microscopic spiders dropped down from it into our teacups. Daddy was phlegmatic about them: 'Improves the taste', he said, carefully fishing corpses out of his teacup.

Maids came and went, but two were permanent fixtures all the

109

fourteen years we lived there. Rose, a stout elderly woman, was head of the dining room waitresses, and had a strong romantic streak. 'Ee, you make a lovely couple, Miss Winifred!' she said after spying on me dancing at a winter Ball with a distinguished barrister in whom I had no romantic interest. The other maid of long standing was Ada, very short of stature and uncertain of age, who was the Hall's sewing maid. Mother once asked her what else she did besides repairing linen. 'Oh, I have my little duties, Madam,' said Ada with a toss of her head – another phrase that was always used by any of us when we asked one another what we were up to. In the War my Father was walking home one night in the black-out, up Cumberland Road, in almost pitch blackness as he had no torch, when he heard a strange and alarming noise approaching him. He paused: out of the inky gloom Ada flashed past him, skipping, 'Goodnight, Sir,' she carolled as she passed on down the hill.

Life in Leeds took us away from the fierce east winds of Newcastle, and deposited us one hundred miles further south, in the centre of England. I had forgotten how miraculous Spring could be, as the sun beat down on the fresh green of burgeoning trees, and where one could feel new growth all round. In 1947, when we moved back to Newcastle, I reluctantly had to sell my open car, which was a joy in Leeds but too cold to drive in Newcastle for a large part of the year. At the top of Cumberland Road there was a 'ginnel' leading through to Woodhouse Ridge, where grey squirrels played and the trees turned gold in Autumn. It overlooked Meanwood Valley, and was lovely for walks, especially as one could catch a glimpse of the vicarage where Titus Oates (the man who 'walked out' on Scott's last expedition to the Pole) had lived in his youth. This story always gave me a shiver down the spine.

In the grounds of Devonshire Hall were tennis courts which I and my friends could use in the vacations. We also had fives courts and the best squash court in Yorkshire which was great fun to play on. I suppose the biggest snag in pre-War Leeds was its fogs. Thick grey and yellow in colour, they clogged your lungs and gave Mummy and me regular bouts of laryngitis. Old people in the neighbourhood still wore knitted woollen respirators when going out in fog. Mother once opened the front door to see how thick it was and put her hand out. It completely disappeared in front of her. That was the night Father was lecturing at Boston Spa and the bus he was returning on only got back to Leeds because the conductor walked under a front headlight, a sheet of newspaper over his shoulder which the driver could just see. They reached Leeds in the middle of the night. Maids on their half-day off duty rang Matron from various police stations in Yorkshire where they were stranded and sheltering for the night. I always found dense fogs frightening. A deathly silence fell around you, and any sense of direction seemed to go. All our underclothes turned grey in a day, and the Cavendish Professor of Physics at the University urged those washing curtains never to rinse them heavily as the soap helped to prevent acids in the air from rotting them.

I was too shy to talk to the male students in the Hall, for I regarded them as beings from another world, all very tough and manly. Unlike me their winter costume was not a warm topcoat, but to their usual outfit of flannels, tweed jacket and hat, was added an enormous muffler. A further concession in very icy weather was the wearing of a pair of rabbit skin gloves from Lewis's, price five shillings. This was the male uniform of the time, just as jeans is now the uniform of this generation. I had a small dress allowance after I was sixteen years old (£20 per annum) so I also sported the rabbit skin gloves, which quickly grew bald on the fingers but which gave me great pride.

My education was now based at home, with tutors who came when I was well enough. I began to blossom, for Leeds was my Mecca, and my health improved as we went on trips and picnics into the glorious dales. I began to walk distances, and we twice rented a house in Austwick in the summer, each time climbing Ingleborough. The second time, after a day of scorching sun and strong wind, I was so dehydrated that I drank nine large cups of tea non-stop at a cafe in Ingleton. Mother had stoically sucked a small pebble all day, having read somewhere that that was done by people dying of thirst in the desert.

Uncle Jock always came to us for some part of the summer; the first time he arrived to join us at Austwick was a sight for the gods. He was very short and extremely fat, but even had he been taller he could not have dismounted from the train at Clapham, as the platform was so low, and the drop from the high train so steep. A flight of steps was solemnly wheeled along the platform to the carriage door, as we three stood at ground level, spluttering out good advice. Uncle Jock descended with great solemnity, bowing graciously to the porter.

The shop at Austwick was run by a couple called Truelove: he had been a butler and she a cook. It was a magical village shop, stocked with all the food any human being could possibly want. All efforts to catch the Trueloves out with requests ranging from caviar to stuffed olives were useless – they could always produce them. I was worried about the creaking floor behind the counter as Mr Truelove served me with tea and sugar, but then learnt his wooden leg was the real reason for the noise.

Prior to the War we started going abroad at Easter for our main holiday. The first time was Easter 1936, when we went to Montreux and Lucerne. I shall never forget my first incredulous sight of the Alps, the sun turning the peaks into wedding-cake icing, standing like clouds in the sky. Montreux became our favourite place: there I had the enchantment of seeing the first green on the weeping willows that encircle Lac Léman, the first sight of a lizard scuttling across the path, the first flowering cowslips, oxlips and crocus poking through the melting snow in the Rhone Valley, and the first joy of lying in bed and gazing across my balcony at the grandeur of the Dents du Midi. It was all quite wonderful. Granny had written to say 'the Harrises are staying in Switzerland – give them my love.' By a miracle we found them by accident, staying next door but one to us. The only small fly in the ointment was the lift-boy at the Hotel Beau Rivage who asked me why Newcastle was not in deep snow like Switzerland when we were on the same latitude – and I could not explain it.

We went on from there to Lucerne by a series of small romantic trains with little snow ploughs in front, through the Bernese Oberland, stopping on top of the Brunig Pass for a lunch of long ham rolls. The air there was so pure we wanted to stay for ever. However the next year we went to the French Riveria, to Menton, where our French hotel had ripe oranges to pick in the garden. One day, after walking over the border into Italy, my father was so incensed in Vintemeglia flower market by seeing 'Mussolini, Conqueror of Abyssinia' painted on the walls that he stumped round saying loudly 'Down with Mussolini!' Mother and I followed, beseeching him to be quiet – we were very lucky not to be arrested.

In 1938 we returned to Montreux and this time went on to Lugano, which was festooned with wisteria in flower, the air heavy with its perfume. I brought home in my sponge bag a periwinkle that still flowers in the garden. Back at Devonshire Hall we planted a wisteria on our house, hoping to recapture the charm of the holiday, but it never flowered, however much we cossetted it. At Easter 1939 we were in Cannes. I insisted on taking our gas masks with us, to Daddy's annoyance. But while we were there people were fleeing from their holidays, back home to England. The airport at Mandelieu was commandeered by the French forces. Long lines of African soldiers on foot and on horseback marched with their guns through Cannes up to the Italian border: our hotel manager assured us that the mere sight of them would make Mussolini capitulate. A trainload of soldiers passing through was labelled 'Berlin, via Rome'. But we stuck to our holiday, and I watched water skiers for the first time behind motor boats of 250 horse-power going at forty-five miles per hour.

At Leeds University Father had a much larger staff than he had had in Newcastle, with eight full-time lecturers and several part-timers. They were all based in Education House. The last time I was in Leeds it still stood, looking forlorn in a jungle of functional and hideous concrete buildings. Further along University Road stood Clothworkers Court, which Michael Innes (J.I.M. Stewart) a young lecturer in the English Department used as a setting for his early murder mystery *The Weight of the Evidence*. I have just re-read this, getting great pleasure from linking the book's *dramatis personae* to their real-life characters.

Father's principal lady lecturer, Elizabeth Maria Blackburn, lived at Birkenshaw with her old father. She was an authority on the Brontës, her father having known Ellen Nussey, Charlotte Brontë's friend. After Ellen's funeral he had purchased the sheet music Charlotte and Ellen used when playing duets – this was later given to the Haworth museum. Miss Blackburn told me her father had said that Haworth villagers pronounced Charlotte Brontë as 'Charlotta Bront'. She took us out seeing Brontë landmarks. I was especially entranced with two links with *Shirley*, namely Oakwell Hall, which is Shirley's house 'Fieldhead' in the book, and the churchyard where Caroline Helstone and Robert Moore met so romantically. Father was so inspired by all this he decided to absorb even more atmosphere, so he and Uncle Jock went to stay overnight at the Black Bull at Haworth, hoping to see Bramwell's ghost. They had no luck and found it rather dull, Uncle Jock afterwards bitterly regretting he had left a favourite walking stick there. To anyone who has not been to see Haworth it is impossible to convey the extraordinary atmosphere that grips you when you find the moor still flows right up to the back door of the Rectory, and you realise how the breezes coming through the heather into that draughty and cold house were forever calling to the Brontë girls.

In 1938 I had my twenty-first birthday, amid much excitement. Mother and I went to London and saw three plays in four days, including Rex Harrison in *French Without Tears* and Ian Hay's *The Housemaster*. I bought a dress at Dickens and Jones for my dance (I still have it treasured up). I had a coral-pink new dress made for the tea party we gave at which I made a speech, warning everyone that they might receive another invitation the following year, as Mother the night before had begun to wonder if it was 1916 when I was born. I had a wonderful birthday, including a lunch at Professor and Mrs John Harveys which was attended by a nice young man – the Earl of Listowel, who proposed the toast to me.

I had by now obtained school certificate and higher school certificate, but as I only had a pass in Latin I could not enter the University to do

114

English Literature under Professor Bonamy Dobrée, as I had wanted. I also had a shot at Cambridge entrance, trying to do a year's preparation in three months, but only passed one of the three papers. However, I was eligible for two courses at Leeds University, either conjoint medicine, which would take seven years, or a two year Diploma in Social Organisation and Public Service. I chose the latter, my only fear being that my health would not stand it. Mrs Wilsdon, who was the charming mother of two close friends said: 'Win, you've been stronger lately – I think you'll manage it.' How right she was. I took to student life like a duck to water, and my health improved dramatically. But I insisted to two friends who were doing the same course that they were not to reveal that I lived in Devonshire Hall. This presumably was inverted snobbishness. However, eventually somebody in our crowd in the second year asked me if I was going to the Devonshire Hall Ball, and was crushed by my friend's reply: 'She *is* the Devon Ball!' We had wonderful Balls, twice a year, dancing to Charlie Steel's Band, with a house party of about twelve couples to join in. I went to lots of other dances too – oh the fascination of meeting glamorous men like Gordon Fraser and Derek du Pré, father of Jacqueline (with whom I once won an elimination dance for being the most romantic-looking couple in the room!). The faithful firm of Burns and Potter drove me home – always Mother, in a dressing gown, was waiting for me, teapot at the ready.

A highlight of the year was the Engineers' Ball, for they provided the décor for it in the Union. A pond and a fountain were rigged up for it in the foyer, and big balloons filled with helium were floated up to the ceiling, half a dozen or so ordinary multi-coloured balloons dangling beneath each. Lights played on them and we danced the whole night through. One friend in a fit of devilment seized me for a waltz and did it at double the normal speed, swinging me round corners in a murderous way. I always swore afterwards my feet never touched the ground throughout the entire dance. Twelve of us then all went to his home and had bacon and eggs, the owner of the house lying blissfully asleep in the dawn upstairs, unaware that we had eaten every crumb of his breakfast.

The diploma course that I was doing was a revelation. We had lectures of course, but our redoubtable tutor in practical work, Ida Brown, started us off by arranging outside visits of observation and I was at last able to penetrate more deeply into the reality of the human lives I had read so much about. Our early visits were led by a Sanitary Inspector, whom I suspect wanted to shock us, and who had no thought for the resentful or bewildered eyes that faced us as he stormed clients' citadels, twenty of us in high heels trailing in the rear. Early on we went to visit a house in Lavender Walk, where a family of two adults and three small children lived in two ground floor rooms. I suddenly realised that nowhere in those bare rooms was there a single drawer and that the family were wearing all the clothing they possessed. Most likely the children were sewn in theirs for the winter, as was the local custom, and which became only too apparent when later the wartime evacuation took place. Round the walls were stuck precious children's drawings brought home from school, so there was love there. We found the same pathetic evidence of pride among the families we met living in barges on the River Aire. After that we explored Leeds slums which looked clean in daylight: it was at night that the bed-bugs emerged in their myriads from the floorboards, furniture and bedding. Later in my career I walked through bugs that crunched under my shoes, and have seen, on a hot summer's evening, whole families sitting or lying on the hot pavement outside their house which had become an unendurable hell-hole.

We then progressed to visiting registered Common Lodging Houses. The Church Army had theirs as a work hostel, where twenty-six men were housed free overnight and then chopped wood in the morning for an hour or so, so that bundles of firewood could be made up and sold by the Army. We liked this plan: we felt it preserved some dignity for the nomadic. We did not like the Salvation Army hostel nearly as much. There the stench in the dormitories was so powerful one of our number nearly fainted and the 246 beds were placed as near to one another as the law permitted.

'Keep your skirts tightly wrapped round your legs, ladies,' roared the Sanitary Inspector. It was these visits that first roused my interest in and compassion for the tramps who then moved relentlessly round the country, many being mentally ill or physically sick, and all penniless, for the state system ignored them unless they settled down into a workhouse. This, of course, to many of the nomadic was the equivalent to prison.

We also visited industrial concerns to observe factory conditions. We had a day in Montague Burton's great factory at Leeds. There were ten thousand employees turning out mass-produced inexpensive suits, and working conditions were excellent. I knew Sir Montague, for he was a Life Member of Leeds University Court, and had endowed Chairs of Industrial Relations both at Leeds and Oxford. A little man, he wore brown kid gloves which he never removed when he attended the big university lectures. We also went to Rowntrees of York for the day, and sat all the intelligence tests their employees had to take when applying for a job. We were all given a free box of chocolates when we left.

I had a placement with Alf Cookes, the printers, who *inter alia* printed Waddington's playing cards. I was stationed with the welfare officer and helped to sell overalls to the workers for small weekly sums, and to administer simple medicines to the sick. Two weeks after I got there the welfare officer became seriously ill, and I had to cope on my own for the rest of the placement. Never can they have had so green a helper, my only noteworthy action being to insist on sending a young man home sick when he obviously had influenza and a high temperature. I did get a letter of thanks from the Directors at the end of my placement, though I would have preferred it if one of them had been to see me whilst I was working alone for them.

Observing children's homes was on my menu too. The Church of England Waifs and Strays Society ran an orphanage in Headingley which horrified us all. It was a gloomy building, the paintwork dark brown, the walls also dark, and the lighting dim. The entrance hall was dominated by the biggest oil painting I had ever seen of ships

117

sinking in battle in a raging sea. The sitting rooms and dormitories were all floored in brown linoleum. In the recreation room the children sat on forms at the sides of long tables. There were no toys, and I asked the Matron why the small glass-fronted bookcase was locked. 'Oh, they ask for a book if they want one,' she said and returned an evasive reply as to how often that was. Solitary confinement and the birch had only just been abandoned. Our whole group found the atmosphere so Victorian and unhealthy that one of our number, whose father was a Vicar and who knew various London officials of the Society went home bursting with indignation to tell him about it. It was closed shortly afterwards. It was so differeat from Headingley Orphan Homes, run by Mrs T. Edmund Harvey and where my mother was on the committee and where the children had unlimited love, and pets to play with.

Near the end of my course I went for a week to Knaresborough to assist in running Knaresborough House, where some twenty wives of the unemployed were sent weekly for a holiday. They ranged in age from twenty to seventy-five years and my daily terror was lest some of the fatter ones went in a rowing boat on the river and drowned. After two days my experienced supervisor left me in charge for the rest of the week, and I had to take morning prayers (wishing I had listened to Auntie Gertie more carefully!), say Grace before meals, produce an entertainments programme whether it be wet or fine, and generally act as mother confessor. The excellent food was provided by a permanent staff, but to my surprise every one of the women guests automatically took a large dose of McLean's Stomach Powder every night. On one awful occasion when we went to Harrogate for the afternoon, everyone carrying a packet of sandwiches, I had to find a café that would let us eat our own food in it, if they provided cups of tea. To my surprise I found such a place, with dirty marble-topped tables, near the station. I should not have been so surprised for I had learnt earlier that Harrogate had some dreadful slums, well off the tourist track. Mary Miller, of the Yorkshire Association for the Care of Cripples had taken me to meet some of her cases, lying pallid and uncared for in wretched circumstances, but in the café I kept hoping that no one I knew would come in. Father was on Harrogate Education Committee, and if Mother and I went over with him in the car he joined us at Betty's cafe for tea after his meeting, so I was not used to 'roughing' it in the Spa.

My happiest placement was for a fortnight with Miss A.K. Baumgartner in the Personal Service Bureau, which had opened in October 1938 to act as a clearing house of information and a casework service for the people of Leeds. She taught me all I knew about casework, but certainly I started at the deep end. At that time a machine for deep radium treatment for cancer had been installed at Leeds General Infirmary, and patients were sent to it from all over Yorkshire. Scarborough Council of Social Service used to ask us to visit and help patients from their area who were staying in rooms in Leeds for their treatment. One woman I saw had not eaten for a week – she had a breast tumour and the radium had burnt her flesh raw. Another case was in lodgings in Leeds; her husband in Scarborough was looking after their three children and sending her seven shillings out of his thirty-six shillings per week unemployment benefit. This was all her income and she used it on dressings for her dreadful burns from the treatment. The Public Assistance Committee refused help because she was not normally resident in Leeds. My task was to get her some additional income from voluntary sources, and also to try and soothe her terror. I visited many cases like these, where agony was etched on faces. I also visited some very quaint people who made a profession of writing begging letters, and I also saw the very poor. I went to a man, wife and six children under twelve years living on £2.5s.0. per week. I visited a hawker and her husband and four children (one of whom was subnormal) living in one room and making wooden clothes pegs for sale. The husband, age sixty-five years, was out of regular work, and the wife, age thirty-nine years, had fainting fits. They always had to keep the window open because of the strong smell of gas in the room. They dared not call in the gas company to repair it, as the bill would go to their landlord who would evict them.

And so it went on, human sadness and frailty appearing in case after case. There was a great need for more medical treatment but not enough money to pay for it. Some doctors had sick schemes, so that those who joined for coppers each week were assured of the comfort of medical treatment when it was needed.

I suppose the most exciting event in my diploma class (if you exclude the famous occasion when we locked the city's Medical Officer of Health, Dr Johnstone Jervis, out of the lecture room) was when Ida Brown imported Dr Clara Stewart to give three lectures to us about venereal disease. In spite of our outward attempts to appear sophisticated, we were mostly unversed in the ways of the world, even though one of my fellow students had announced that she believed in free love: we secretly considered that she was a scarlet woman! But I was learning fast....

At my much-loved home I found many of our visitors engrossing. Sir Wyndham Deedes came often, about three times a year, with people like R.A.H. Livett, the City Architect, coming up to show him the plans for the growth of Leeds. The Bishop of Ripon, Geoffrey Lunt, became a friend and Bishop Leslie Hunter often came over from Sheffield to see Father. They were only two of the numerous bishops who came, Daddy getting them to meet and talk informally with students. Eleanor Rathbone MP made us a regular port of call, and in turn we visited her in her London house in Romney Street, where she lived with Elizabeth McAdam. Eleanor took us on my first trip to the House of Commons, where I heard Churchill speak, and sat at the next table to Jimmy Maxton at tea. Colin Sharpe, headmaster of Abbotsholme School in Derbyshire, came often, for Father was chairman of the governors there. Cyril Burt came – but Father did not trust him. Lady Allen of Hurtwood and Diana Forbes-Robertson also came. Names flash through my head, all of people who died long ago. The most regular visitor was Uncle Jock (The Revd. J.O. Kennedy) my Father's Cambridge friend who was almost one of the family.

We went to an international conference in Oxford in 1934 that was the first in the world to examine the problems and experiences of British and foreign university teachers. One hundred and thirty-three delegates came from forty-four universities. Father was president and opened the proceedings. G.D.H. Cole turned up wearing a red tie, which was quite exciting, and I got Madame Maria Montessori's autograph – no mean feat as she spoke no English, and I no Italian, and in any case I do not think she was keen on the idea. One sunny afternoon there we went to Foxcombe Orchard, on Boar's Hill, to have tea with Lt. Col. and Mrs Radice. Sheila Radice was the deputy editor of the *Times Educational Supplement* for which Father, for years, wrote most of the front page articles and leaders. When his book, *A History of English Elementary Education, 1760 – 1902* came out in 1931, he had rushed to get the *Times Educational Supplement*, and he and Mummy turned eagerly to the reviews. There was nothing there. You could see the disappointment as he folded the paper and turned away. 'Look!' suddenly shouted Mother, and there – the whole of the front page was devoted to the review! We all had a warm feeling for Mrs Radice, but I became additionally grateful, for I had from her my first lesson in imaginative flower arranging. We walked into a sitting room in her house where on an old oak table a very low black circular bowl was stuffed full of very short-stemmed flower heads of every colour – a great splash of magnificence. By the fireplace stood a big green glass transformer case with huge branches of yellow roses in it. The art of flower arranging was in its infancy, and I copied both ideas as soon as we got back to Leeds. I could not replicate the flagged walk that was bordered on each side by a thick hedge of lavender, full of bees, nor could we ever have achieved the trees of ripe plums growing up the tennis court netting, so handy for a quick snack in a game.

We had many close friends in Leeds, particularly the Wilsdons and Professor and Mrs E.O. James. The latter and I wrote blank verse to one another which still makes me chuckle when I read it. She had a lovely sense of humour, and once told me that anywhere more like a parochial meeting than Monte Carlo Casino she had never seen! Pre-War, every Easter and Summer vacation the James' loaded their car with linen, silver, the cat and the cook and drove down to Oxford where they had a house in Kennington. I stayed with them after the War when Professor James had just become Chaplain of All Souls, as well as Professor of the History of Religion at London University. I much admired the way he had poured a watering can full of weed killer through the weeds in his garden to make a path, for at the time he could not get a gardener. He took me round the Oxford colleges; he drove with complete disregard for other traffic, talking all the time and describing what we passed. I sat by him cringing with fear, as irate cars hooted at us, and people shouted.

Leeds was a superb centre for the arts; not only had it got an Academy Cinema at which we saw all the Leni Riefenstal classic films, but it was also the home of a very good theatre. The Leeds Grand Theatre had all the latest plays with London stars, a great favourite being Cicely Courtnedge and Jack Hulbert (Father had been at Cambridge with him, but to my fury never knew him). We found, in the war, that if you took a box in the theatre you could order tea and HAM sandwiches to munch in the interval, in the secrecy of your box. This was a glorious extra meal in wartime.

In addition there was some exceedingly good repertory work. The Peter Powell Players, where the principal stars were Mr Powell's wife, Jean Anderson, and Ruth Wynn Owen. They introduced us to plays like *Kai Lung* and *The Moon in the Yellow River*. In our local cinema we rocked with laughter at the superb antics of Ralph Lynn, Tom Walls and Robertson Hare in the Aldwych farces: it was a golden era of entertainment that did not bring a blush to the cheek.

This too was a golden age of literature, and I read all the newest authors – and a lot of the old ones too. I loved thrillers (made respectable by the rumours that they were eagerly devoured by the clergy) but I tackled anything from heavy biographies to history and light novels. Magazines, too, abounded and they introduced me to my developing deep love of birds and the countryside. Not only did we take the *Countryman*, but after a man called Harry Scott called at the University to see my Father to ask him if he would subscribe to a new magazine he was starting, called the *Dalesman*, we took that too. Pre-

122

War England, although the storm clouds were gathering, was full of adventure in the arts. We used to go and examine exhibitions of art and sculpture at Temple Newsam, where Philip Hendy was trying to interest Leeds in modern art. What a pity we did not buy any, for it was oh, so cheap! Henry Moore puzzled us, as did a lot of the pictures. Mother was greatly relieved to find that she had guessed correctly the title of one painting. It was 'Plaice on Chair'. Sometimes the titles and the subject seemed to bear no resemblance to one another, doubtless due to our lack of appreciation of artists like Paul Nash, etc.

Chapter Twelve

Leeds 1939 – 1947

The summer of 1939 was a perfect one of hot sun and blue skies, yet we were always dashing indoors to listen to news bulletins on the radio. The first night of the War when the air raid warning started we all rushed to the cellar to find it full of bustling cockroaches. 'Never again,' said Mother, thereafter going into the drawing room during raids, her only concession to Hitler's henchmen being to wear a felt hat as a protection against possible bombs (she always wore one in bed during thunderstorms too, in case the chimney came down).

The advent of war changed the pattern of our lives. The maids left the Hall to go to munitions, and an army of dailies took their place. The blackout blotted out the cheerful lights twinkling across the lawns from the students' rooms, and Miles Archibald, a barrister and member of staff found it more difficult to serve the small and select crab suppers he gave in his room to those favoured with an invitation. The evacuation of eighteen thousand, two hundred and fifty Leeds schoolchildren took place on 1st September 1939, and going through Hunslet in a tram I saw dozens of weeping women hanging on the railings of a school, and waving goodbye to their offspring who were being taken to the safety of the countryside. Each small figure had its gas mask slung over its shoulder. Long after the war I talked with Dame Eileen Younghusband about the traumatic effect evacuation must have had on the younger generation, for however carefully cushioned they were at the time, the break with home must, in innumerable cases, have damaged the bonding with their parents: trust must have been broken. Perhaps even now, in the current mindless hooliganism of a new generation, we are reaping the result. The rigours of war were followed by the biggest unnoticed revolution of all – the post-war demolition of communities as bulldozers razed slum streets that had for generations cushioned the occupiers against a harsh world. People post-war lost the security of their family units, and of living close together. It is difficult to quantify damage done to personalities, but perhaps history will reveal the true story.

When I came downstairs from my last examination in June 1940 I had no idea what I was going to do. I and my friends had all said we would take up nursing, but luckily most of us eventually stayed on to complete our diplomas. At the bottom of the stairs stood my tutor, Ida Brown. 'Win', she said, 'would you like to go to the Personal Service Bureau for six weeks, three to be with Miss Baumgartner to learn what to do, and three to run it while she has a badly needed holiday?' 'Yes', I replied, and went along to the Bureau to see Baumie, whose office was in Blenheim Terrace, in the basement of the Yorkshire Ladies' Council of Education. I rushed in. 'Miss Brown's asked me to come and look after here while you are away,' I said. An expression of absolute dismay spread over her face, for both she and I knew how inadequate and unsure of myself I was. I realised Miss Brown had not told her I was coming, so we had an awkward few minutes together.

I passed my examinations, Mr Shimmin, the director for the diploma, even crossing the road one day to tell Mother of his pleasure at my papers. Some time afterwards Father told me that it was the custom in Senate for those present to clap when the names of any staff children were read out in the examination results. It must have been the first time he had ever had occasion to feel proud of me, for usually it was his lecturers' children who were the achievers! Never in all their lives were my parents critical of my lack of success. Three professors' daughters passed the diploma in 1940 – Eve Jones, Elizabeth Milne and myself.

So I went to the Personal Service Bureau to do the casework, and to run an office. Our premises consisted of one large room, with a most able typist in one corner, and me in another. Mrs. A.S. Turberville, the honorary secretary of the bureau, came in for my first morning alone on duty and positioned herself casually in a third corner, where she could hear everything. I am sure she shared Baumie's doubts about my proficiency. My first client was an appealing young woman asking for money – the Public Assistance Committee would not give her any out-relief, and she said she was destitute. I had money in the desk drawer for emergencies, and her story moved me – until my nervous eye fell on her legs, which were clad in a beautiful pair of nylons. Now I knew that nylons were scarcer than gold, and only odd pairs reached Leeds smuggled in from the USA, so I hardened my heart and sent her away. 'I never had another scrap of worry about you,' said Mrs Turberville as she left. I did not point out it was sheer luck, engendered in me by all those years of illness and reading detective stories by Sayers, Cole and Crofts that had given me a small capacity for looking at problems, probing and reasoning until I could produce a solution.

A Citizen's Advice Bureau had been incorporated in the Personal Service Bureau soon after its inception, and between 1939 and 1945 it dealt with twenty-eight thousand, nine hundred and seventy-one enquiries. In addition the number of cases Baumie and I handled was two thousand, seven hundred and thirty-three. When I left the Bureau in 1947 it was reckoned that I had dealt with at least ten thousand people. For I stayed there not for six weeks, but for seven very happy years. For the first two years, looking on it as War work, I accepted no salary, but in my third year I let them pay me £50 for the year – they had practically no money anyway.

Baumie became a great friend. She was a descendant of Pepys and her father, whose ancestor had been a friend of William Tell, was Medical Officer of Health in Newcastle upon Tyne for some years in the last century. She was an Oxford graduate who, in the First World War, entered the women police force, later becoming a moral welfare worker in London. She was a person of the highest integrity and intelligence, and one instinctively trusted her fairness and kindness. She worked often in the office until after nine at night, going back to her flat to find it cold and foodless, but she survived. Once when she collapsed from influenza I took her home in a taxi and Mother and I nursed her, refusing to allow her to smoke any cigarettes, to her fury. She retired to Muker in the Yorkshire Dales, but she had over-strained herself and the elasticity in her lungs gave out. She died at Ambleside in 1965 devotedly nursed by her sisters.

In 1940 the Red Cross Postal Message Service (twenty words for one shilling, transmitted to enemy territory via the Red Cross) grew so large that Mrs Turberville took charge of it, helped by a band of volunteers, including Miss Elaine Barron, Miss Nance Pflaum and Mrs Edward Arnold. They transmitted 31,357 messages and replies during the War. They enjoyed their work, seizing on any light relief they could in the darkest days, as for instance when they had to send off a message from a young girl to her parents in Germany: 'Had a beautiful baby boy. Will explain all later.' A large proportion of the messages got through, bringing untold happiness, but a lot met increasing lack of response.

Leeds in war-time was transformed. Many of the smaller factories changed from the textile trade to making machine tools and weapons in prodigious quantities. Corporation officials worked wonders at promoting plans to ensure the City kept running as smoothly as possible. Mr Burton of the Housing Department was made Billeting Officer, and on the first day of war commandeered and had swept out a small shop that previously sold bird seed at 107 Portland Crescent. For months one crunched on the floor, but he and his staff were ready for anything, day or night, for he also had the steps to his front door there outlined in whitewash – an innovative idea at the time. The Lord Mayor's secretary, by name William Pitts, also took on the additional duty of Food Officer, going across to another office at 5 p.m. each day, where he had a different secretarial staff. The city was full of unsung heroes with whom I worked closely, and where comradeship was the order of the day. I even learnt from a Public Assistance

Officer how to make toasted cheese on an electric fire. In short, the city worked hard and uncomplainingly, and was ready for anything.

Citizen's Advice Bureau work meant knowing national and local war-time regulations about anything from bomb damage to starting a pig club, from how to get extra clothes coupons to how to get bananas for a child suffering from coeliac disease. It taught me a lot: you never knew what would come through the door. Once a lame man, leaning heavily on a stick, limped in. 'I want to speak to the Secret Service people at once – I'm Lord Avebury.' He pulled out his identity card, and I recognised that this was an emergency. I at once dialled a service number I had, and with great reluctance, but full of loyalty to Crown and Country, left the room so that he could talk in private. I never knew what it was about, and shall die still consumed with curiosity. His daughter-in-law later became a great friend, but she could throw no light on it.

At other times the utterly pathetic would come to the office, like the man who bought a house with all his savings, and then discovered it had no lavatory! The vendor had neglected to tell him that he had been friendly with a nearby publican who allowed him to use the pub facilities. The new owner and his pregnant wife were then forbidden this favour. I got an Elsan chemical lavatory placed in a small bedroom, and an arrangement with the Local Authority for its contents to be regularly emptied into a street drain.

During the War Leeds became a reception area for evacuees from London, the most famous being my friend Millie, a Russian Jewess. She was an ex-cook, in her sixties, and came from the Mile End Road where she had lodged 'mit Luxemberg and his nineteen children'. In the bombing there she had lost the contents of a wardrobe most precious to her. It seemed to have elastic walls, as each week she remembered more of its contents to add to her compensation claim to the War Damage Commission. They at last rang me up in despair: I urged them to settle her claim as soon as possible, for I too was wearying of the saga. She had a daily routine of visits, going first to the Assistance Board pleading for help in her very incomprehensible

129

English, whereupon a poor harassed official would ring me up, begging me to see her. I always weakly agreed, for I had a soft spot for Millie ever after she told me Leeds was full of 'Teefs, beglars and prondestooters' – a marvellous phrase and, at the time, very true. Once, after many invitations, I went to have tea with her, carefully averting my gaze as she poured milk into my teacup from a basin a scraggy-looking kitten had just had a good drink from. Eventually, after the War, she was repatriated to London: within a fortnight a telegram to me arrived at the office. 'Come at once. Am in trouble.' Regretfully I declined, re-referring her to the Family Welfare Association to whom I had already entrusted her.

The biggest group I dealt with in the War were the British War Refugees from overseas. Leeds was the official reception area for the whole country and housed them in Quarry Hill Flats, furnishing each flat with basic essentials – one cup, one knife, one spoon, one bed, one sheet etc., per person. Mr Burton and his staff rang me as soon as someone arrived from France, Italy, the Far East, Tangiers and the Channel Islands. I went to see them at once, even on a Sunday, often with an interpreter if the new arrival knew no English, to find out needs. My office was the agent for the British Council for Aid for Refugees which was based in London, and we were able to get grants to assist them to settle. I had to solve such problems as where to get a tyre and inner tube for an invalid chair made in the Far East, where to get a woollen body belt and a square feather pillow etc. The British War Refugees were a very mixed group, ranging from a Chinese girl married to a British Tommy who was so high in caste she had never dressed herself, down to depressed elderly and unsuccessful artists and governesses from the French and Italian Rivieras. Some had been in the concentration camps and friction was caused in a group if there was any suspicion that there had been fraternisation with the Nazis. Nearly all these 585 overseas refugees were in a state of shock and despair and had to be helped to find their equilibrium. Many were separated from spouses or children, and desperate for news that never came. Quarry Hill Flats had much sadness in it during the War, for earlier 600 troops had been billeted there after Dunkirk. I can still see those blank exhausted faces staring through the windows: seeing a broken army is something one never forgets.

So I was extremely busy, not only in the office, but in doing home visits. In the War it was very hard after dark finding houses when your torch in the unlit streets had the regulation two layers of tissue paper over the bulb. I once was doing an urgent visit for the Royal Naval Barracks at Portsmouth, where a rating was waiting anxiously for a report about the severity of his wife's illness in Leeds. I got off a tramcar in Hunslet Moor in pitch blackness, and my torch gave out. I heard footsteps and appealed to an unseen figure for directions as to how to reach the address I was going to. It was a man. 'Over this grass is t'shortest,' he said. 'Take my arm.' We hitched up amicably and plunged across a large piece of wasteground, eventually emerging at some houses. 'Ee,' he said, 'it's a long time since I had a lass on my arm!' We parted with mutual good feeling, but my Mother expressed horror when she later head the story. I told her to be calm, for it got me to the house I was seeking.

I had a set-back in 1943 when I collapsed from overwork and for four weeks had to be at home. I had been very torn in my mind as to where my duty lay, for the ATS had got in a bad way, and Eleanor Rathbone had been at our house and tried to persuade me to go to help to re-organise it nationally. Mother said she could face anything as long as we were all together, and although she did not forbid it, I decided to stay in Leeds and continue my work there, but I suffered agonies of conscience in making the decision.

Princess Mary, the Princess Royal, came to the office to praise and encourage us. Once she came and stood in the back of the room to listen to me interviewing an elderly Cockney, bombed out in the East End, but wanting to return there. The next time I saw him I asked him if he had known who had come in. 'Why bless you, yes!' he said. 'When I had my oyster stall I always used to go to Buckingham Palace to open their oysters at a party!' I always wondered if this was true. Princess Mary was very much part of the Leeds scene: I have seen her

131

shopping, unrecognised, with Christmas crowds in W.H. Smith's. She was always so generous with gifts for our work.

The Duchess of Kent came in 1943 to receive a cheque for £13,103 collected by a special Fund for the Starving Children of Greece. Mrs Turberville had been chairman, and I represented the young people of Leeds on it. Archbishop William Temple had dined with us for the first time a couple of nights after he had officiated at Princess Marina's wedding to the Duke of Kent, and I had asked him if she was as pretty as the photographs suggested. 'She is the loveliest thing I have ever seen,' he said. It was a joy to look at such beauty and for years I saved the white glove I had worn when I shook hands with her.

Archbishop Temple was a wonderful man. He used to come to have dinner in Hall with the students, afterwards spending the evening talking with them in their rooms. He was very popular, and had a superb and unique laugh, that boomed out of his vast frame, and which once so convulsed our pair of usually silent maids when they were serving him at dinner, that Mother had to send them out of the room. Stories about him were legion and treasured. Mother and I once saw him extricating himself from the passenger seat of an Austin Seven, outside St John's College in York. Somehow one leg got left behind, and every time he tugged it the whole car moved forward. He used to spend his holidays in the Lake District (we were booked into the Fish Hotel at Buttermere, on his recommendation, when the War broke out, and had to cancel) and there was a supposedly true tale that when staying there he sent a surplice to be washed. The local washerwoman sent it back with a note pinned on it: 'To washing One Bell Tent, 1/9d'.

My home life was still busy – it could and did happen that when I got home at night (usually at 7p.m.) Father would tell me that Mother's laryngitis or rheumatism was bad, and I was to go with him to act as hostess at some function. He once gave me ten minutes to get bathed, and turned out in full evening dress and I managed it! Mother herself was busy with War work. As soon as we got to Leeds in 1933 she had joined the Leeds branch of the National Council of Women, an organisation that existed 'to unite the women of Great Britain in promoting the social, civic, moral and religious welfare of the community.' In 1937 she was made its chairman and began to work tirelessly for it. On 1st December 1938 the branch called a public meeting to inaugurate in the city the Women's Voluntary Service, so that if War came there would be volunteers available for special duties. Two hundred and forty attended and Lettice Cooper was one of the speakers, coming to tea first with Mother. Talks were given to the branch on 'Prisons Today', 'Human Biology', 'National Spinsters Pension Association' and 'Rescue Work in the Diocese of Manchester' etc. Prior to the national Annual General Meeting, the National Council sent to its branches resolutions on social problems that were to be discussed, so that national viewpoints could be obtained. In 1936 there had been 39 such resolutions, and the Leeds branch did not hesitate to raise its voice in protest at this pressure of work.

The advent of war in 1939 meant Mother became enmeshed in much more NCW work. She led a campaign to increase the number of women police in Leeds, in order to cut down vice and immorality among young girls. It was a slow battle, and many areas in the country had shown antagonism. By 1944 Leeds still only had two policewomen, and 43 unattested WAPCs (without police powers and therefore only doing clerical or canteen work). Yet Leeds was by then banned to members of the American and Canadian armed forces on leave, and was notorious for its prostitution. The regional office of the National Council of Social Service was situated in a street opposite the home of one of the most prosperous brothels: the staff used to watch the taxis decanting their customers at its door. The owner, reputed to have made £60,000 out of the War, was at last put in court on a minor misdemeanour – that of showing a light in a blackout. The story ran round the city that she had stepped into the witness box, quivering with righteous indignation, and announced that they couldn't do this to her as she was under police protection. I learnt a lot about prostitutes, realising quickly that a social worker should never visit certain houses in the morning – the occupants would still be asleep in bed. I worried about what would become of a small peaky nine-year-old who at night had to be frequently awakened and put on the floor under the bed, so that his mother could entertain her client on the mattress above. At an amusing level, a friend of mine, waiting on the steps of the big Queen's Hotel in City Square for her doctor fiancé to join her, was surprised to be jostled by a girl in the blackout who muttered: 'Move on, this is my patch.'

Mother brought in big guns for her campaign. Public meetings were held, and Mother kept up a brisk correspondence with press and public. Lady Lawson Tancred, the Hon. Mrs Gwendoline Peel, entered the fray, along with Viscountess Halifax. The latter was president of the Leeds branch, and letters flowed into our home from the British Embassy in Washington and 88 Eaton Square. She was wonderfully supportive and kind about all the branch's activities, and after I told her I collected autographs, she sent me John Masefield's.

By the end of the War the branch was exploring the need for more hostels for unmarried mothers and arguing that small foster homes were preferable to institutional care – a very far-sighted view. But Mother was not only involved in the NCW. As I have said, she was on the committee of the Headingley Orphan Homes, which Mrs T.E. Harvey and the committee ran on faith, and a deep belief that somehow they could continue to pay their way. They were a wonderful example of determination in a just cause. Mother was also attached to the Spring House Home (Leeds Ladies' Association for the Care and Protection of Friendless Girls). Also before the War she had been an inaugural member of the Woodhouse Open Air Nursery School in which she was deeply interested. She was also on Leeds Safety First Committee, which discussed the need for more safety on the roads, especially for children. The Leeds NCW enlivened it by sending them a resolution to discuss urging the need for a bye-law forbidding motor cars to pass a stationary tramcar on the nearside, and suggesting that trams should carry a red rear light to enable the driver to notify following traffic when the tram was going to stop. Mother also, somewhat to her surprise, became president of the Leeds Girls' Friendly

Society in the Diocese of Ripon.

Mother had started a student dramatic society at Devonshire Hall, and every year they put on a show of three one-act plays – great searches were made to find plays with an all-male cast. Nothing deterred her: deciding that one English student called Lesley Sands was so outstanding he should meet some professionals and get their help in a stage career, she hauled my Father one night round to meet Emlyn Williams in his dressing room at the Leeds Grand Theatre. Mr Williams was kindness itself, and helpful. In the War the society still flourished, though performers sometimes were called up, and performances had to be in the early evening before possible air raids. On one occasion the guests included Lord Harlech, the regional commissioner (i.e. liaison officer between the army and the civil authority: able to take over in time of chaos if government broke down), his ADC, the Hon John Freeman, and the vice-chancellor, Dr Mouat Jones, all of whom we knew well. In one quiet and poignant scene on the stage a loud whirring noise was heard in the distance. (The dish washer in the Hall's kitchen was old). Our three principal guests tensed themselves ready to rush off. Lord Harlech and his ADC were billeted with Bernard Mouat Jones in his house in the next road and we often heard in the night the roar of cars as they rushed to Command Headquarters as enemy aircraft approached. We, too, had a link with the warning system – our night porter was a friend of the night porter at Leeds General Hospital, who rang him every time the infirmary had a red alert as enemy planes crossed the coast. We were on the flight path for planes going to bomb Liverpool and Manchester, so our nights were very broken. Mother would fill the electric kettle and we would settle down to read or knit until another call from the infirmary gave us the 'All-Clear'.

Leeds itself was surprisingly clear of raids, except one fearsome night when we were bombed for six hours. Factories in Hunslet blazed on each side of the railway line as T. Edmund Harvey MP's train inched its way nervously into Leeds station. The following day, to get to work, I had to climb over garden walls to avoid soldiers with fixed bayonets standing guard over unexploded bombs in Headingley.

The memory of the daily tragedies that surrounded us is very clear. Of close friends I suppose the first to be killed was Flying Officer John Wilsdon, who at the age of twenty-one volunteered to lead a bombing raid on France in 1943 and was shot down over the channel. Mother and I went to see his Mother shortly afterwards, and going into the house saw one of John's great friends, Flight Sergeant Louis Aaron, lying white-faced on a sofa. He had called to see John and had only then just heard he was missing. Louis, also aged twenty-one, went back on duty and in the August was captain and pilot of a Stirling aircraft detailed to attack Turin. An enemy fighter's fire shattered their windscreen, hit three engines, and put out of action the front and rear turrets. The plane became unstable, the navigator was killed and other members of the crew wounded. A bullet struck Louis, breaking his jaw and tearing away part of his face. He was also wounded in the lung and his right arm was useless. The plane dived, and control was regained by the Flight engineer.

After being given morphia Louis was lifted back into the pilot's cockpit: too weak to take control he wrote orders with his left hand. Five hours later the plane landed with its bombs jammed on board, and its undercarriage retracted. Nine hours later Louis died. He had earlier been awarded the DFM but died before he was told: now he was awarded the VC posthumously.

The War years and just after were exhausting. The domestic front at Devonshire Hall changed – nearly all the maids were called up into munitions. The redoubtable Ada was transferred into serving in our house. Rationing and shortages furrowed brows in the kitchens: one Christmas Mother longed to produce some festive cheer, and arranged for us both to go in next door to Mrs Wilsdon's for a grand cookery evening. She would herself, she announced, make a cake, for she had an egg Dr Morton, the headmaster of Leeds Modern School had given her, and which she had treasured for just such an occasion. Dr Morton had a caravan in the Dales, and just occasionally was able to give us an egg which Mother usually beat up, raw, adding sugar, brandy and a pint of hot milk, thus producing sufficient for three glasses of nectar for us.

Off we went to the Wilsdons, Mother carefully carrying her egg. Came the time when she tapped it on a basin to break it, and it exploded with a loud bang, and the kitchen was filled with the most noxious fumes. Mother collapsed in tears, the Wilsdons and myself in loud hoots of laughter.

My other cookery memory is of Dorothy Keeling, who was the national organiser of the Citizen's Advice Bureaux, coming to stay with us one night. I had just read a recipe for Wartime Truffles and made some on which Dorothy and I fell with great avidity. The mixture was mashed potato, mixed with cocoa powder, rolled in little balls and then in more cocoa powder. After about the fourth we both felt most dreadfully sick, and Dorothy retired to bed and was seen no more that night. Luckily my parents had both refused them.

Father had been incredibly busy, introducing an extra fourth term in the Education Department's year, in order to train teachers more swiftly. He and his staff even ran a school in the Education Department at a time when Leeds schools were closed and there was nowhere for the students to carry out school practice. In streets round the university plenty of children had crept back from an unhappy evacuation, or because bombing had been lighter in the city than expected, and they were bored and longing for school. In his last few years at the university Father was Pro-Vice Chancellor, during which time Dr Mouat Jones, the Vice-Chancellor, was often absent on various government commissions, so Father had to run the university moving back and forth between offices with different sets of secretaries. Along with Canon Cockin he was adviser to William Temple, now Archbishop of Canterbury, on the future role and work of the Church Training Colleges. Once when he was going to stay with the Archbishop, I dimly heard him leave the house very early in the morning by taxi. He had no sooner gone than my Mother rushed into my bedroom – 'He's forgotten his clean collar!' she said dramatically. As Mother always sent us far too early for trains (I once caught the one before the one I was meant to) I hurled on my clothes and ran all the way down the hill to the tram. I arrived at Leeds Station with about two minutes to spare. It was at a time in the War when no one was allowed on a platform except those actually travelling, but I pushed past the ticket collector at the barrier, waving in his stupefied face the precious collar in a bit of white tissue paper. I shouted 'I must go on the train – it's his clean collar!' I then had to search the train which seemed full of sleepy-looking elderly men, all reading *The Times* or the *Yorkshire Post*. At last I found Father, who must have thought he was dreaming as I thrust the collar in his hand, and got off just as the train was pulling out. When he got back he said, 'I didn't need it', and we found out he'd spent part of the time with the Archbishop on the floor as buzz-bombs went overhead.

All through the War (and before!) Father presented innumerable prizes at innumerable schools, and in 1936 he had opened the new hall for women teachers at Brighton Municipal Training College. 'Even Shakespeare Couldn't Spell' gleefully headlined the *Brighton and Hove Herald* in what they termed one of his brilliant passages at the opening speech. In 1941 he indulged in crossed swords in the *Yorkshire Post* with the then leader of Leeds Labour Party (the party he always voted for, Mother voting Conservative, so they cancelled each other out). This latter dispute had blown up over a meeting of Leeds Class Teachers Association, and whether it was political or not. It was holding a meeting to discuss the provision (or lack of it) of Air Raid Precautions at the city's schools. The speaker was the Bishop of Bradford (Dr A.W. Blunt, famous for having let the cat out of the bag about the Duke of Windsor and Mrs Simpson); Father was chairman. The leader of Leeds Labour Party accused them all, in strong terms, of being tainted with communism. This was a bombshell to poor Dr Blunt, who rang my Father in a terrible state. Luckily Father had initially wondered if it was to be a political meeting, so before accepting the chairmanship had asked the organisers this very point. He was told the meeting was not political. The press had a field day, and Father was rather amused, and the Bishop and he gallantly stuck to their guns. Every pronouncement on education that Father made was fully reported in the press, both locally and nationally.

One day, after chairing a meeting in Bradford, he and mother drove J.B. Priestley and the first Mrs Priestley back to Leeds. On the way Father discussed where to retire to – this was a topic he and Mother talked of endlessly. The Priestleys were most interested. A year later, just before we left Leeds, we went to see *The Linden Tree* at Leeds Grand Theatre, with Sybil Thorndike and Lewis Casson in the main roles, and we sat in our box, Mother and I with the tears rolling down our cheeks. Priestley had obviously got his idea from that car ride, and although parts of it were quite different it struck home very sharply at times.

We were all tired for during the War we only had one week's holiday a year away from the Hall. Twice we went to Ilkley and twice to Bolton Abbey, where the Rector and his wife took in the War-weary as paying guests. The Rector was an old Emmanuel College man from Cambridge so he, Uncle Jock and my Father greatly enjoyed gossiping together. One afternoon we were joined for tea by a nice young man in uniform – the Marquess of Hartington, soon to marry Kathleen Kennedy, and eager to come to see Devonshire Hall for his father, the Duke of Devonshire, was Chancellor of Leeds University. It was bliss to go on long walks, and even to sit motionless in the garden. The Hall, adjacent to the Abbey, was housing the evacuated Leeds Girls High School and, at dusk, before the bats came flittering round our heads, small groups of girls strolled about or sat on rugs reading in the last rays of the sun. An oasis of peace lay round us, and enabled us to recharge our batteries for the next year's ceaseless round of work.

At last came 1944 when the Allied invasion of France took place. Poor Mother, how unkind we were at breakfast on that June 6th! It was her birthday, and she opened the *Manchester Guardian* to find that after innumerable rejections they had at last printed a short poem from her. But Father and I had no time for her – we were listening avidly to the news from Europe in which she was temporarily supremely uninterested. *The Guardian* paid her 10s 6d for her effort.

In 1946 I was staying with Baumie's two sisters near Ambleside in the Lake District when at breakfast the maid came in to say I was wanted on the phone. It was Mother. 'Win, we've been asked to a Royal Garden Party at Buckingham Palace on 16th July and Daddy says he won't go!' I sent him a pithy message and of course we did go – and in 1947 as well. It was a most thrilling experience, and I've wanted to drink iced coffee ever since. To me it was particularly exciting as because there had been no presentation parties during the War, any daughters who accompanied their parents to the 1946 Garden Party were deemed to have been presented at Court. So I was a deb at last, besides being 'one d.' in *Who's Who*. The 1947 Garden Party was also memorable. I had left my famous £25 car at Leeds Station and offered to give a lift home to Bernard Mouat Jones, the Vice-Chancellor, who had also been at the Garden Party. He accepted eagerly, for it was nearly midnight and not a taxi in sight. Dr Mouat Jones' step flagged a little at the sight of my car. I got my parents in the back, but there was no room for my guest's 'topper', as the roof was too low. He sat with it scrunched up on his knee, and I set off up Woodhouse Lane. Half way up the cover fell off the boot, and clattered behind on up the road, hanging on the flex to the car's one rear light. The noise was stunning, but we carried on, rehearsing what we would say to the police if we were stopped. I think the Vice-Chancellor was glad to get home. My only previous problems with the car had been when turning it briskly into a side street and immediately being enveloped in clean sheets and washing hanging across the lane to dry.

Later in 1946 Father felt slight pins and needles in one arm, and a pain in one leg whilst he was lecturing. After a few days he told Mother. Doctor was called, and immediate rest prescribed. I took my parents on November 11th to see a consultant, Dr McAdam, and waited in my little car at the door. After half an hour Mother rushed out. 'Daddy's dressing,' she said. 'Dr McAdam told me he's very ill – he may only live a week.' We gazed at one another speechlessly for a long minute, then she turned and ran back indoors. He had had a slight

140

stroke, but only his secretary and the Vice Chancellor were told. To his astonishment he was told to take three months off work.

In 1947 Father retired at the age of 65. We returned to the house we had lived in before in Newcastle. This complete severance from Leeds was of course misunderstood by some, but we felt that only less stressful surroundings could help him, when he would be well away from the fifty-six committees he sat on, and on which he held a good percentage of chairmanships. Many people did not realise what the strain had been on him. All through the War students we had known and liked had disappeared, never to return. Then in 1942 a Portuguese engineering student, living in Devonshire Hall, shot himself. He had made an earlier attempt to poison himself, but my Father had spent a lot of time with him and had got the Hall's student committee to help the man, who spoke little English.

Father felt it very deeply. Then, not long before we left Leeds, not only did the head gardener drop down dead, but a Devonshire Hall student was drowned when boating on the Wharfe. It was nine days before the body surfaced, and again Father was inwardly distressed, although he never revealed his grief. Mother was the strong one, coping with police and the grief of relatives. In retrospect it was easy to see how the pressures of the last few years had affected my Father, and started his decline in health.

Father had begun to resemble David Lloyd George more and more, especially if his hair wanted cutting. Strangers came up to him in hotels to remark on the likeness – I wanted him to send his photograph in to a film studio to get a star part. When we moved back to Newcastle he retained his chairmanship of Abbotsholme School. He had great love of independent schools, and this one was very close to his heart. He had for years been a governor of Leeds Girls High School and Leeds Grammar Schools, which he represented on the Governing Bodies Association. Another more recent Governorship was at Giggleswick School. He was particularly pleased that another new governor, joining at the same time as him, was young Lord Shuttleworth, a descendant of the old Lord Shuttleworth he had

TEL. NO. 20251

THE UNIVERSITY,

LEEDS. 2.

1st October, 1947.

Dear Smith,

I have pleasure in informing you of the following
resolution which was passed by the Senate at its meeting today:-

"On the occasion of his retirement from the Chair
of Education the Senate wishes to place on record its
recognition of the signal services to the University of
Professor Frank Smith. Since he came to Leeds fourteen
years ago, momentous and complicated developments in
national education policy, added to general wartime
problems, have made the work of an education department
more than usually difficult. Professor Smith guided and
fostered its growth with a sagacity of judgment and a
generous devotion of energy which won the warm regard of
all his colleagues. He brought the same qualities to
the work of University administration, whether as chairman
of numerous committees, member of Council, Chairman of
Board of Faculty, or, lastly, as Pro-Vice-Chancellor:
but his concern for sound academic administration never
interfered with his warm human interests or sympathy in
the personal welfare of individual students, to which
his thirteen years of responsibility as Warden of Devonshire
Hall also bear impressive witness.

In his outside activities Professor Smith rendered
the University notable service through the relations he
established with teachers and educationalists of all kinds
in the city of Leeds, the West Riding, and beyond. He
was widely and warmly esteemed as a man of ripe scholarship,
humane and genial wisdom, firm but conciliatory, and
generous in giving help to all who sought it. He was a
most valued counsellor in many civic and philanthropic
causes.

His colleagues wish him in his well-earned retirement, complete restoration to health and many years in
which to pursue in congenial ways his varied interests in
the cause of education."

May I add my own good wishes that you and Mrs. Smith
will thoroughly enjoy the new-found leisure of your retirement.

Yours sincerely,

Professor F. Smith,
76, Moorside South,
Fenham,
Newcastle-upon-Tyne.

Registrar

known so well, and worked so hard for in his early days. We moved back to Newcastle in October 1947.

Chapter Thirteen

Newcastle upon Tyne, 1947 -

Returning to Newcastle, back to a semi-detached five-bedroomed house in a street, was quite a challenge. We had meant to go to Surrey, but my Father's exhaustion curtailed our chance of exploring there, so we gave our tenants in Newcastle notice, and to our surprise found that they were already planning to retire to the West coast, so they left. We congratulated ourselves that when we went to Leeds in 1933 there had been a slump in house sales in the North East, and we had been forced to let our house, rather than sell it at a reduced price of £1,450. It was a godsend, for just after the war houses were scarce, and the fact that we would return to the same doctor, neighbours and shops was wonderfully comforting. Everything pivoted round my Father. I left my job as assistant secretary of the Leeds Council of Social Service three months before we moved, so that I could help with the task that lay ahead. Everyone had thought that I would succeed Baumie as secretary of the Leeds Council of Social Service, for we had worked together to build up the original Personal Service Bureau into the Council, but not everyone had realised that Daddy was retiring, and ill, and there was no question of the family separating. The Press made a fuss, presentations and tributes poured in to all three of us, and removers were booked. Eventually, on 25th September 1947, Father drove Mother, me and our highly nervous cat, chittering with fright in a borrowed cat basket, the ninety-nine miles North to Newcastle.

Later that night we fetched from the station our ever-faithful Mary, who sped from Wales to help us. She stayed three weeks with us. She had never been out of Wales before, and when we met on the platform I found out we had forgotten to give her our Newcastle address! 'I knew you'd be there,' she said. When we took her on country rides she was entranced by the different shapes of the haycocks in the fields, while in town she kept asking 'Where do all these people come from?' This was a phrase I heard later from Sid Chaplin when he and I were giving opening talks at the University to a new intake of Applied Social Studies students. The latter came from all over the country, and our task was to give them some background to Northern life. Sid used to give a superb account of life down the mine and of how, as a young pit boy, he came into Newcastle for the first time and how incredulous he was at the sight of so many people.

We settled in happily, though it was much colder the hundred miles further North, and for the first time Mother and I had to battle with food rations. I dug the garden and planted it with gooseberry bushes, raspberry canes, and Grandpa's famous rhubarb crowns, all of which we fetched from Wood Villa. To start with we had a three week holiday in the Lake District, going in my £25 car, which even stuttered its way up to the top of Honister Pass, to Father's enormous delight. He knew by then he could not walk up it again, and that the walking holidays he had revelled in there with Uncle Jock were a thing of the past.

After three months at home, my parents were so horrified at the sight of me scrubbing a floor that I returned to work, and we were able to afford to employ a cleaner, Father's pension not being very large. I became Family Caseworker for Northumberland, under the Northumberland and Tyneside Council of Social Service, for a modest salary, for in the War most of their voluntary donors had disappeared, and the staff had been reduced from sixty to five. Some time later, under pressure from the committee, my Father resumed his chairmanship of the NTCSS. He had kept on his work for the Council of Church Training Colleges, his chairmanship of Abbotsholme, and was an external examiner for the Durham Colleges and the region's training colleges.

Although Father was frail, his personality had not begun to disintegrate. However, after 1949, when he had another slight stroke, his irritability increased. In 1950 he had outbursts of rage and excessive worry about money, though he behaved normally in front of visitors. Mother and I knew however that he was changing, and my heart nearly stopped one morning when he wrote a letter and asked me to look at it to see if it was all right. His command of English had always been impeccable, and to realise that after so many years he had become unsure of himself, tore at one's very being. In June 1950 his reactions in conversations slowed down, but he could still chair meetings with vigour and skill. At home he sat with his head in his hands, and stopped reading.

In August he accused Mother of stealing money, and that evening fell in the garden when picking raspberries. At 1.20 a.m. in bed, he started breathing stertorously. For twelve days he tried to get out of bed day and night, and giggled a lot. He became incontinent, but tried to improve, as I continued at my work, rushing home to wash at least nine sheets a day. He had a month in hospital when he saw the chimney pots outside his ward window as human figures. The consultant confirmed that oedema (water on the brain) had set in, and only deterioration could follow. He came home and had no interests, even on rides in the countryside he loved. In the November he actually proposed a short vote of thanks to the Duke of Northumberland at a meeting: Mother had written on a card the two words 'stimulus' and 'inspiration', and Daddy used these two words almost to excess.

On 27th January 1951 he woke confused, and as fast as he was dressed he undressed. He demanded breakfast in the middle of the night; we had to lock all the downstairs doors and hide the keys to prevent him going out, sometimes semi-naked. All reason went at times. He ate and ate, though the offer of a pot of tea often calmed him a little. His speech nearly went, and back he went to hospital. 'Where does the fundamental path go?' he kept asking. Again he came home; there was talk of certification, as drugs could no longer control him. I thought I found him trying to electrocute himself and he told me 'If I was my father's son I'd put an end to all this'. He cursed me and accused us of poisoning him. Nurses came so that Mother could rest a little, for we were up day and night, but he wanted Mummy all the time. He had a heavy stroke on April 9th, his only words after that being 'It's absurd, absurd, absurd' and then to the doctor 'Please, please.' He died on 11th April 1951. I was sure then, and still am, he knew what was happening to him during that last year of sadness.

My Mother, who had shown incredible bravery throughout, was inwardly now like a lost soul. Her photograph shows a face that is sad – and lonely. We had wonderful friends and help, but how easily can one repair the damage when part of your life goes away? I heard Mother saying 'We are no longer a trio' – but she kept going, as Grandma Prichard and her own mother had before her. Father, Mother and I had always adored one another, though Daddy was very undemonstrative. I remember once in the war he called me 'Dear', and I left the room shaking and thinking 'He loves me!' It was two years after his death before my grieving for him came to the surface. I collapsed going to work, and had to have two months at home, when I could not eat or sleep. Aunties Annie and Edith were most concerned, and paid for a holiday.

My recovery was gradual but helped enormously by joining an evening ornithology class at the University. This was accompanied by field outings (at one of which I broke my leg), and residential weekends. I got used to creeping out in the middle of the night to lie in snow-encrusted heather on the moors watching and listening to a Blackcock Lek. Have you ever been dive-bombed by an Arctic Tern on the Inner Farne Islands off the Northumberland coast? It is very therapeutic.

Before Father died my job had enlarged. In 1948 the Family Welfare Association, in London, persuaded the Carnegie United Kingdom Trust to grant-aid an enquiry into the need for a family casework service in rural areas. I was seconded by the NTCSS to take charge of the Northern part of the experiment, in Durham and Northumberland. Helped by an advisory committee, I carried out the enquiry.

I took a questionnaire round a random sample of one-tenth of the population in selected parts of both counties. I had the help of Flora Beck in analysing the findings, for it was the first time I had had to be absolutely certain about the validity of statistical returns, in order that they were foolproof in the final report I was to write. I met dozens of people in both counties, sometimes getting back to Newcastle late at night: once from South Durham with the exhaust broken on my car. Helen Bate, carrying out the Southern part of the project in Oxfordshire, used different testing methods. It took twenty-one months of continuous work for me to produce the final report. Dame Eileen Younghusband, the chairman of the whole project, and Ben Astbury, organising secretary of the Family Welfare Association, were very supportive.

The results showed that as many clients in the countryside needed a casework service as those in towns, but of course the figure had previously appeared to be much less because fewer people lived in rural areas. It was nice to have sound evidence, and the report contributed to many discussions up and down the country at a time when professional interest in social work was stirring, and universities were becoming more involved in social work training. I myself spoke at conferences in Edinburgh and Carlisle, besides all the local publicity.

In my early days in social work, my professional body, the Association of Family Caseworkers (eventually absorbed by the British Association of Social Workers) used to have an incestuous system whereby a trained practising caseworker and a university lecturer went jointly to the different casework agencies to test out their proficiency in giving practical training to students. I was used in this way, and at different times inspected the Edinburgh, Glasgow and Aberdeen Councils of Social Service. It was helpful – one picked up new ideas and learnt a lot, besides ensuring that students were going to get good practice placements.

People have very largely forgotten how disdainful local authorities were about the voluntary social services. The latter were seen as 'do-

149

gooders' whose hearts ruled their heads, and also because local authority committees and staffs were jealous of the freedom of the voluntary societies, who were not answerable to ratepayers, and who could carry out experimental schemes. Had I not heard the Leeds Personal Service Bureau, then doing splendid pioneer work, referred to as 'a Wartime mushroom growth' by the then Director of Public Assistance? In 1948 I sensed the same attitude present on Tyneside when I joined the staff of the Tyneside Council for Voluntary Service. In those days social workers were nearly all women, paid small salaries, and there was no career structure. I found an organisation that was very different from the pre-war think-tank I had known as a girl, when Henry Mess, as director, had shone like a comet on Tyneside. It was obviously important that a body so broken by the war had to achieve better relations with the local authorities if it was to survive; luckily Northumberland County proved co-operative, and in 1952 set up, with us, the Northumberland Family Care Committee, which employed a caseworker to do intensive work with 'problem' families in Blyth and Bedlington. In addition they grant-aided me. I sat on many joint committees, acting as advisor to County Health Visitors.

At the same time I was acting as 'Personal Welfare Organiser' for the Northumberland and Tyneside Council of Social Service, for in 1954 Evelyn Davison, who then held that post, had left. The first day I sat in her office I faced a large room completely dwarfed by every wall being lined with cumbersome old furniture. This had come to us from the nine branch casework offices the NTCSS had previously run and were now closed. On the shelves thirty-two antique wire baskets stood, their torn wires making your hands bleed over the dusty files they contained. All were marked 'urgent', and awaiting a home visit. There was just space enough in the centre of the room for a small square carpet, on which stood the desk at which I sat. As my back was to the door, I speedily altered the arrangement for after dark, when I was working alone in the building at night, the stairs creaked alarmingly as the building cooled down.

By day I dashed about in a small Ford car, and people said that except for a few hospital almoners and probation officers, I was the only social worker between Tweed and Tees! This was not Evelyn's famous GBB car – that had a life and notoriety of its own. Alec Trotter, head of the Rural Community Council, was disconcerted when driving it, to find that when he put his arm out to signal he was turning right, the whole window frame slid up his arm and hit him smartly on the ear. The brakes were never of the best: once with foot brake and handbrake full on I glided straight across a main road from a side road – luckily at a moment when there was no traffic about. GBB's rear light was erratic too, and when it failed one night Evelyn had to put a torch in the back window of the car, after carefully coating the bulb with her lipstick.

I had to run a sub-office at Gateshead and South Shields, trying all the time to offer a specialist service to the public. As I was organiser for Citizen's Advice Bureaux on Tyneside I decided to spend my Gateshead time re-opening the CAB there, with a trained voluntary staff. The local authority had assured me that their officers could handle any problem that came their way, and I had a struggle to convince them that, for example, a clerk in the Town Clerk's office could not solve a matrimonial breakdown. For South Shields we eventually got another caseworker, with the help there of the Medical Officer of Health: she worked closely with his department. Luckily on 1st July 1954 J.D. Long had come as organising secretary of the NTCSS, and was determined to rebuild it into the leading voluntary organisation that it once had been. He had imagination and flair, and gradually improvement came, and the status of the office improved. He left me to run the casework, and we shared some of the rest of the work, but he was the one who handled the big problems of the Council's role in economic and strategic matters in the region. The late Duke of Northumberland, our president, was no figurehead, and responded generously to any appeal for advice.

Evidence was given to the Local Government Commission on Tyneside in 1960, and we also tackled a knotty problem that worried voluntary organisations greatly – would they lose their independence if they got grant-aid from their local authority? A regional conference on the Younghusband Report on the training of students was the forerunner of many conferences through the years – on poverty, on old people's welfare, on various Government reports. I gave evidence to the Parliamentary Select Committee on violence in marriage, and crossed swords with its chairman, Mr Willie Hamilton, MP. I was secretary on Working Parties on Fuel Debts in 1967, and this led me into being a member of a small delegation organised by the National Council of Social Service that spent a morning in London with Tony Benn, then Minister of Energy. I also started taking delegations of Newcastle social workers, both statutory and voluntary, to meet the top officials of the local gas and electricity boards in order to discuss ways of helping our clients to pay their bills. The boards had a great dislike of fixing pre-payment meters in houses because the most improvident always seemed to have them smashed open just before the meter was emptied. We had to get them to relax this policy in particular cases of hardship, and with mutual discussion much progress was made. I found that top officials often had no conception of what it meant to live on a weekly income and expenditure basis, in a home where a quarterly gas or electricity bill could represent an insurmountable problem. One board was proud of the fact that anyone – 'But anyone, Miss Smith' could walk in any bank and pay their bill over the counter. Blank incomprehension greeted the fact that most of our more improvident or unlucky clients had (a) never been in a bank and (b) were too terrified to try entering one. But it was all very good tempered, and both sides found our discussions helpful. My reward came recently when I was hailed in the street by one of the officials who told me that his board had the lowest cut-off rate of its supply in the country. He was sure that it was due to the duologues that we started years ago.

In Newcastle, I was chairman of the Octavian Club for many years. It met monthly and attracted social workers to a tea meeting with a speaker. An off-shoot was a study group of which I was secretary. We agonised about casework theory at evening meetings in one another's houses. When Newcastle University planned the post-graduate Applied Social Studies course in 1960, it was this group of about nine social workers that formed the first band of practical work supervisors for the new course.

Miss A.K. Lloyd, then head of the social studies work at the University planned the new ASS course, and gave brilliant and inspired leadership at a time when it was badly needed. Generous to a fault in letting others get praise that should really have gone to her, she was the anchor in a programme that brought great credit to the University and the City. The course too was fortunate in its appointment of Miss A. Watson as its lecturer in Social Studies. There were other tutors who made impressive contributions to the course, including a delightful American, Miss Dorothy Pettes. I was amongst the first group of practical work supervisors that the University appointed as Associate Teachers in Social Work, which gave me particular joy remembering my father's earlier Professorship on the staff. How pleased he would have been to see my name in the University handbook!

The North East was of course brought up on the coal fire, but re-housing schemes meant families had to learn how to use other methods of heating and cooking, although many tried to cling to the open fire. In the coal strike of 1972 the miners in the area would only deliver to a house where there were special needs and where the coalhouse had been inspected by a social worker. I called together thirteen volunteer non-statutory social workers and we visited 221 homes in Newcastle in four days, in an effort to help the city's social work department, which was swamped with cries for help. It was incredible seeing coal houses in Newcastle without even any coal dust in them, so desperate was the situation. It had its brighter moments as when one of my staff was in a house when the grandmother of the home walked in and deposited on the hearthrug an enormous bundle of park railings. 'Here you are, pet,' she said.

Brian Roycroft, the director of Social Services for Newcastle, has achieved well-deserved recognition. A facile and interesting speaker, highly skilled in negotiation and management, he has never lost his respect for individuals, and makes time to talk and help those who face difficulties. He can cut red tape, but if he does so he knows why, and can argue a reasonable case. In the coal strike he was seen delivering coal from his car to those in need.

Working in homes where poverty reigned made me recognise more and more how handicapped the poor are in the tools they have to work with. I kept telling my students to be aware of this, for I was constantly finding homes where there was only one pan or one pie dish to cook in. In one case I found five children eating milky porridge off flat plates with forks – the only eating tools they had. (This explained the stains on the wallpaper). I visited three of our women's clubs (relics of the clubs for the wives of the unemployed), begging them to recall how they had produced simple meals in the days of mass unemployment, or during the rigours of war. They found it an absorbing exercise. I was able to produce a cookery book, giving recipes for dishes that could be made in one dish, or even on the oven shelf. We also started a cookery class, for many of our poorer clients, and used an ex-Guide mistress as teacher, who was used to practical problems in camping. I had found domestic science teachers were no good for what I wanted. She was a great success.

Such pieces of work were recorded in the NTCSS's annual reports, and usually attracted the attention of the media. I was on television both locally and nationally, and interviewed by such well-known people as Harold Williamson, Frank Bough (Mother called him 'Chuff' as she could not reconcile the pronunciation of his name with its spelling), Michael Rodd, Alex Glasgow, Jake Kelly, Tom Kilgour, Mike Neville, etc. They seized gleefully on such stories as that of the old man who felt too poor to contemplate buying new spectacles, and who read the evening paper with the aid of an empty glass goldfish bowl. Tilted carefully, it met his need for magnification of print. The press too used my stories, and occasionally the serious or the tabloid papers sent special reporters hot-foot to Newcastle. The most exciting was my brief comments in 1966 on illegal back-street moneylenders, and the exorbitant rate of interest they charged. Reporters and a photographer arrived immediately from London, begging me to give names and addresses, which I of course could not do. I sent them to Newcastle's West End, and they got their story without difficulty. Hot on the heels of it being printed, one of the moneylenders bounced into our office, angrily threatening us with a court case. As we had never even heard of her it was really very amusing – although not to her.

Other causes I took up were the plight of the homeless, the alcoholic and the mentally sick. I was involved in the formation of various committees, including NECA (the North East Council on Addictions) Newcastle MIND (Newcastle Association for Mental Health) and Northern MIND. With Bill Utting I organised overnight counts of those sleeping rough in Newcastle, using the result as a launch pad to get better facilities and, just as importantly, a wider understanding of some who choose to 'sleep rough'.

My main work, though, was in the training of students and in 1964 the Joseph Rowntree Memorial Trust granted us sufficient money to run a training unit for five years. It enabled us to appoint other trained casework staff, and at one point I had five exceedingly loyal, gifted and hardworking professional colleagues with me, in particular Pippa Kellner, Edwina Mallinson, the late Elsie Winch and Marie Ellert. A fortuitous visit to the office one evening by Sir Keith Joseph, in 1973, then Secretary of State for Social Security, led to grant aid to the unit from the Department of Health and Social Security. Sir Keith had come to attend a meeting of the Northumbria British Association of Social Workers, of which I was chairman, and had told me to write to him about our financial headaches. This we did, and he was an enormous help. When I left Newcastle Council for Voluntary Service in 1981 (the NTCSS had been renamed) we had had 283 students for training in our unit. Usually they had come for a period of four and a half months, for two days a week, with some parts of it as block placements.

In May 1974 another chapter opened in my life. Statutory and non-political Community Health Councils were formed, in order to represent patients' views to health authorities and the NHS. I was already involved in health work as I had been made a member of the Wansbeck Hospital Management Committee in 1970, but now I was elected vice-chairman of the Newcastle Community Health Council, becoming its chairman in 1981. A whole new world opened up. Vast forests in South America must have been felled as National Health Service reports flooded into my home. Luckily Newcastle CHC had as secretary Vera Bolter, whose intelligence and flair for the work clarified the largest problems. It was obviously fatally easy to condemn a health service scheme on presentation, without appreciating all the complex network of hospital and health provision that might then be affected. In 1974 Newcastle had thirteen hospitals, including one big teaching hospital which had a regional function, besides numerous clinics etc. Many CHCs only have one hospital in their patch, so obviously our work was going to be heavy. In some areas of the country the relationship between the health authority and the Community Health Council has been acrimonious, which is sad. Sir Michael Straker and his successor Arthur Taylor, and their officers, have listened with the greatest courtesy and fairness to Newcastle CHCs proposals, comments and criticisms. They appreciated the amount of work the members and staff spent in research among the public, in order that arguments were well-balanced between the patients' well-being and the practicalities of a solution. At our statutory annual meeting between health authority and CHC the chairman and I each chaired half the meeting – an ordeal for me in case I disgraced my side!

I suppose an early success on the CHC front was over our success in interesting Sir Michael Straker, then chairman of the Newcastle Health Authority, in the great difficulties experienced by the homeless in getting medical care. The chairman of the Family Practitioner Committee and I had already argued about it for an hour as he flatly refused to have 'these dirty people' in or near his surgery. At a meeting with Sir Michael I discussed this gap in medical care, with the result that when a conference was called in Newcastle by Single Homeless on Tyneside about the problem, Sir Michael brought some of his chief officers along. Now we have a city-centre drop-in medical and psychiatric facility that caters admirably for a most difficult group of patients. I am sure the health of those addicted to a nomadic life in the North-East has improved considerably.

The attitude of the health authority's officers to the mechanics of closure has now changed, but in 1974 the CHC went to inspect Walker Park Hospital, in Wallsend. Originally donated to care for men injured in shipyard accidents, it had just been closed as redundant. The yards were closing, and also certain injuries were better cared for in new specialist units in other hospitals. The staff had already scattered to other posts. An official unlocked the door, revealing what must surely have been a blueprint for the interior of the *Marie Celeste*. Paper, test tubes and equipment were abandoned on benches, as if someone had blown a whistle and everyone had rushed out. There was a tap running, and a noise from above was traced to two men actually stealing lead from the roof. Our guide tut-tutted and rang the police to come and collect the burglars. The CHC stared in horror at the unkempt rooms, but the worst blow of all was that the full medical records of the patients treated there were also lying loose on desks, for anyone to read. At that time the health authority had no experience of closure, but this experience sharpened their approach to it, and never again did the same thing occur.

The conferences and meetings I organised were legion – one can do a lot of work in a twelve hour day. During my Mother's last year of life in 1967 she did not realise how often I was at home in the evenings, and that I was not going to meetings in London nearly so often. When she died on 5th December my first act was to write to Uncle Jock for help: he was part of the family – and a vicar! – and he had come to Mother and me after Father had died. I wanted him. On 7th December I was alone in the house and checking the obituary column in the *Daily Telegraph* to see if they had printed Mother's entry correctly, when my eye lit accidentally on a name higher up the column. 'On December 2nd, suddenly, the Rev John Oswald Kennedy...' I sat there, shaking and crying. I was the only one of our quartet left.

After Mother died I evaded grief by cramming more and more work into my day. I was on twenty-three committees and acted as secretary of the Council for Voluntary Service's Golden Jubilee celebrations in 1978, but in the June I awakened one morning completely blind in one eye. I felt no pain, but the consultant diagnosed a hypertensive retinopathy. With rest the sight returned, better than ever. In June 1980 I had a severe pulmonary embolism which left my lungs scarred. This was due to a deep vein thrombosis: a relic of breaking my leg in 1955. Since 1980 I have been on a strict daily dosage of Warfarin. In January 1981 I had a gallstone operation. This had threatened earlier, but I was hoping to delay it until I retired. I made history – I had a three and a half inch gallstone stuck in my intestine, and lost one and a quarter stones in weight in twenty-four hours!

In the Birthday Honours list in 1977 I was awarded the MBE, and had the pleasure of making my fourth trip to Buckingham Palace, and of talking to Her Majesty the Queen, to whom I had been presented when she came to Newcastle in 1974. On that occasion she was opening MEA House, a purpose-built building of offices for voluntary services, and which was the brainchild of J.D. Long. I had the responsibility of temporarily furnishing our open-plan office there so that some seventy staff and tenants could meet Her Majesty. This event really set the pattern for my contacts with Royalty, for in 1982 when I was chairman of the Newcastle branch of Save the Children Fund, the Princess Royal came to attend a children's concert in Newcastle Cathedral and I was the hostess. My Save the Children Fund contacts had also brought me into contact with Countess Mountbatten, and tea with Mr and Mrs Attlee at 10 Downing Street.

I have been associated with Save the Children Fund from my Leeds days: in Newcastle I at once joined the local committee, becoming honorary secretary. Soon after, Mrs Alington, wife of the Dean of Durham, suggested that her relative, Joyce Grenfell, should give a one-woman show in aid of the Fund in Newcastle City Hall. This and subsequent joint events necessitated visits to the Deanery. Mrs Alington was charming, decisive and great fun to be with. She had a faithful and enormous dog, its huge frame dwarfing that of many visitors. It was called MU after the Mother's Union. Every time MU died they levied 1d fee on all members in order to purchase the next MU. One day at tea I suddenly discovered that my gloves had disappeared, and it became all too apparent that MU was crunching something in the darkness under the dining room table. Urged on by Mrs Alington I went on hands and knees under the table which was of such size that I completely disappeared from view. With difficulty I wrenched my gloves from MU's reluctant jaws, and turned round to crawl back into daylight and Mrs Alington's concerned smile. She was the youngest daughter of the fourth Baron Lyttleton (I think he had seventeen children) and she used to say how glad she was that her father had not heard of birth control!

In 1986 Her Royal Highness the Princess of Wales came to open new headquarters for the North East Council on Addictions, and I made all the arrangements – by then I was known to police and sniffer dogs!

Royalty has generously come to Tyneside many times in recent years, but I was especially thrilled to meet Princess Alexandra, for we had a talk about her mother, HRH Princess Marina, Duchess of Kent – the Fairy Princess whose marriage I had discussed with William Temple so long ago.

Envoi

As I re-read what I have written I realise I have missed out such a lot I could have included; long-forgotten faces and events keep leaping into my memory in a tantalising way. I wonder too whether I have recorded the right material to convey to the reader the strengths and weaknesses of my family background, and the impact on all of us of the places in which we have lived. I have tried to convey a picture of a life that has largely vanished: whether for the better is a matter of conjecture.

'Noble work is the true educator' wrote Samuel Smiles, and 'The mind must be awakened by knowledge'. I have tried always to learn and to work hard in what is, after all, only a fleeting moment of time. Most of all I have tried to learn humility and not to be such a snob as I once was. I have listened to, and never ceased to marvel at, the courage exhibited by the sick, the elderly, the lonely and the poor. They bear burdens far harsher than any I have experienced. I am lucky that in all my being there burns a sure conviction that the glories of nature are one of the signs of an omnipotent presence: never shall I forget the day when, in 1936, I dissected a bud off a beech tree. To see, cradled in silky hairs, the minuscule leaves ready for the following year's growth, was a revelation. It was my first conscious appreciation of the way the universe was planned. The scent of a flower, the perfection of a landscape, or the miracle of glorious prose or verse – oh, I do so hope and pray man does not despoil them more than he has done already!

The years have brought me countless friends, and for that I am eternally grateful. To them I dedicate this book, as a small token of appreciation. Some have often wondered about my background – well here it is.